To DeVoraH sHosHANAH Kayl

HAPPY HANUA

THE MYSTICAL DIMENSION

Volume III:

CHASSIDIC DIMENSIONS

CHASSIDIC DIMENSIONS

Themes in Chassidic Thought and Practice

by

Jacob Immanuel Schochet

KEHOT PUBLICATION SOCIEY
770 Eastern Parkway Brooklyn, New York 11213
5750 ● 1990

Copyright © 1990
BY J. IMMANUEL SCHOCHET

All rights reserved.
No part of this book may be copied or reproduced in any form without permission from the copyright-holder, except for the quotation of brief excerpts in reviews

THE MYSTICAL DIMENSION
Volume III:
CHASSIDIC DIMENSIONS

Published and Copyrighted © *1990 by*
KEHOT PUBLICATION SOCIEY
770 Eastern Parkway Brooklyn, New York 11213
Tel. (718) 774-4000 ● 493-9250
Printed in the U.S.A.

נדפס בדפוס
שמחה ובנו גרשון גלוקאוו
BOOKMART PRESS, INC.
N. BERGEN, N.J. 07047

נסדר בדפוס ״עמפייער פרעסס״
ע״י מרדכי ליב בן פיגא וויוסף יצחק בן ברכה
EMPIRE PRESS
550 EMPIRE BLVD. ● BROOKLYN, N.Y. ● (718) 756-1473
FAX (718) 604-7633

ב"ה

Dedicated

בדו"ר

לכ"ק אדמו"ר
the Lubavitcher Rebbe
שליט"א

whose personification of all the ideals
discussed in these pages
inspired their writing
and motivates their emulation

Marking the 40th anniversary of his blessed leadership
we beseech the Almighty to grant him the strength
to continue guiding the people of Israel toward their destiny
and to lead all of us toward Mashiach
very speedily in his and our days
בגאולה האמתית והשלימה

Chassidic Dimensions

Table of Contents

Preface	9
Foreword	15
כלל גדול בתורה: The Dynamics of *Ahavat Yisrael*	17
וצדיק יסוד עולם: The Concept of the *Rebbe-Tzadik* in Chassidism	81
"Serve G-d With Joy..": On Overcoming Anxiety and Gloom	125
Religious Duty and Religious Experience in Chassidism	151
Lamplighters: The Philosophy of Lubavitch Activism	179
Bibliography	217
Indexes	221

PREFACE

Over the course of the past few decades I was invited to deliver numerous lectures about the history and teachings of Jewish mysticism, and particularly of Chassidism. At the same time I also published a number of books, essays and studies in those fields. By virtue of the great and increasing interest in Jewish mysticism, many people have urged me for years to gather and publish these lectures and essays in one depository for ready access.

For most of the lectures, however, I have at best very brief notes of key-words and some references, except for those that were recorded by listeners. Also, most of the articles and essays, written over the course of close to three decades, are in need of updating or revisions. The great amount of time and effort required for producing transcripts, and for editing and revising all materials, prevented me from undertaking this task. On the other hand, there are troubling strictures relating to "He who withholds 'corn'.."

(Proverbs 11:26), as interpreted by our sages.[1] Thus I started gradually with a selection of materials for which there has been a greater demand, to produce this initial series of three volumes on the mystical dimension in Judaism.

The essays and studies in these volumes deal essentially with explanations of the mystical tradition and perspective in general. The emphasis is on themes and topics that are both central and practical in Chassidic thought. Most of the material was revised, and updated with references to presently readily accessible editions of sources. Occasional overlapping of some themes and ideas is to be expected. More often than not, however, these "repetitions" complement or supplement one another. In view of the fact that this is a collection of essays and studies composed at separate and varying times, there is disparity and inconsistency in the transliteration of non-English words and the rendition of names (e.g., in some parts *Rambam*, and in others *Maimonides; Joseph* and *Yosef*; and so forth).

The copious footnotes should not scare off the average reader by giving the appearance of a technical text. These volumes do not represent original insights of the author. They are no more than an attempt to present ideas and teachings of old. Most of the notes thus simply present my sources. Other notes explain or qualify the text, or offer further elaborations.

The numerous quotations from, or references to, Talmud, Midrashim, Zohar, and early classical sources, are not intended as a display of erudition. They simply demonstrate

---

1. *Sanhedrin* 91b. See *Zohar* III:46b; *Sefer Chassidim*, section 530, and the commentaries *ad loc. Cf. Rosh Hashanah* 23a; *Sukah* 49b; *Vayikra Rabba* 22:1; *et passim.*

how the cited teachings of Chassidism, especially its alleged innovations, are firmly rooted in the historical tradition of normative Judaism.

The modern trend is to put footnotes at the end of chapters, or of the whole book, to avoid the appearance of an overly technical text. Personally I find this awkward. Taking advantage of an author's prerogative, I applied my preference for footnotes in the margins of the relevant passages to more readily serve their purposes.

In view of the intended aims of these volumes, the citations of Chassidic thoughts and teachings generally concentrate on the original sources of the early masters, more particularly — the teachings of R. Israel Baal Shem Tov and his successor, R. Dov Ber, the Maggid of Mezhirech. Bibliographical details for texts cited appear in the index.

The mystical tradition is the most delicate part of our Torah. Thus it is the author's fervent prayer to be spared of errors in this undertaking. By the same token he hopes also that these volumes will contribute somewhat to the goal of illuminating the world with the light of *pnimiyut Hatorah*. This will of itself speed the Messianic promise of "The earth shall be filled with the knowledge of G-d as the waters cover the sea" (Isaiah 11:9), "and they shall teach no more every man his neighbour and every man his brother saying, 'Know G-d,' for they shall *all* know Me, from the least of them unto the greatest of them" (Jeremiah 31:33).[2]

J. I. S.

---

2. *Zohar* III:23a; Rambam, *Hilchot Teshuvah* 9:2, and *Hilchot Melachim* 12:5.

Bibliographical notes for The Mystical Dimension

Volume One: The Mystical Tradition

"To Be One With The One": Combination of revised article published in 1971 and transcripts of lectures.

"Jewish Mysticism: Authentic Tradition vs. Subjective Intuitions": Edited transcript of lecture delivered at the International Symposium of Jewish Mysticism, Oxford (England) May 1981.

"Let Your Well-Springs Be Dispersed Abroad": The text of the first seven chapters appeared first in *Di Yiddishe Heim* XVIII:4 (Spring 5737), then with notes as Foreword to the 3rd edition of *Mystical Concepts in Chassidism* (1979). The present edition is a slightly emended version of the original, with the addition of the last three chapters.

Volume Two: "Deep Calling Unto Deep"

"The Dynamics of Prayer": Revised and expanded version of a series of articles that appeared in *Di Yiddishe Heim* V:2-VI:4 (Fall 5724 — Summer 5725).

"The Dynamics of *Teshuvah*": Edited transcript of a lecture delivered at the International Symposium of Jewish Mysticism — Oxford (England) May 1981 — with the addition of notes.

Volume Three: Chassidic Dimensions

"The Dynamics of *Ahavat Yisrael*": Revised combination of part of an article that appeared in *Tradition* XVI:4 (Summer 1977) and a series of articles that appeared in

Di Yiddishe Heim VIII:3-IX:2 (Winter 5727 — Fall 5728).

"The Concept of the *Rebbe-Tzadik* in Chassidism": Edited transcripts of lectures with the addition of notes.

"Serve G-d With Joy..": Revised and expanded edition of an article that appeared in *Di Yiddishe Heim* XXV:3 (Spring 5746), with the addition of notes.

"Religious Duty And Religious Experience In Chassidism": Revised edition, with the addition of notes, of an article that appeared in *Di Yiddishe Heim* XIV:3 (Winter 5733) to mark the bicentennial of the passing of the Maggid of Mezhirech.

"Lamplighters: The Philosophy of Lubavitch Activism": Slightly revised articles that appeared in *Di Yiddishe Heim* XIV:1-2 (Summer — Fall 5733), and *Tradition* XIII:1 (Summer 1972).

FOREWORD

Chassidism is an integral part of *sod*, the mystical tradition of the Torah. It is the well-spring of *pnimiyut Hatorah*, the inner core of the Torah. Thus it casts light on all other parts of the Torah, on *Halachah* and *Aggadah*, illuminating the legal, moral and philosophical teachings of our tradition. It provides a deeper perspective and penetrating understanding of the other dimensions of the Torah, i.e., of *peshat* (plain meaning), *remez* (allusions) and *derush* (hermeneutical interpretations), and even of *sod*, the Kabbalah as a whole.

As an integral part of the Torah-tradition, Chassidism does not innovate. Its teachings and practices are not something new or novel that came into being for the first time with the founding of the Chassidic movement. Every one of them is deeply rooted in the Torah of Sinai. Any aspect of originality lies in new *emphasis* rather than substance. The esoteric is not only restricted by the exoteric, but most intimately intertwined with it to the point of absolute unity. Even as many mystical or Chassidic concepts depend on the exoteric dimension of Halachah or *peshat* for understanding, so there are many Halachic concepts which can be understood only in the context of the mystical dimension.

A fair number of ideas and concepts bear the distinct mark of Chassidic emphasis. In the course of time they have become so current that some no longer realize that they are dealing with a uniquely Chassidic dimension. The concept of *hashgachah peratit*, of Divine Providence guiding and directing every particular detail — in both the human and non-human realms — would be one example of this kind.[1] In turn, there are ideas and concepts that are so strongly identified with Chassidic teaching and practice that some no longer realize that they derive wholly and totally from Talmud, Midrashim and the teachings of the authoritative masters of Jewish tradition.

This volume deals with some concepts of the latter category. Concepts like universal *Ahavat Yisrael*; the figure of the *Rebbe-Tzadik*; the idea of a "Joyful Disposition"; and the emphasis on "Religious Experience"; are so closely identified with the teachings of the Baal Shem Tov and his disciples that they are often taken as uniquely Chassidic. In this volume we shall try not only to explain the Chassidic dimension of these concepts, but also to place them into the historical context preceding Chassidism. Hopefully this will lead not only to a better understanding of these concepts, but also to a greater appreciation and emulation thereof.

J. Immanuel Schochet

Toronto, Ont., 10th of Shevat, 5750

---

1. See *Likutei Sichot*, vol. VIII, pp. 277-284, for an incisive and comprehensive analysis of the concept of *hashgachah peratit* in the history of Jewish thought and philosophy. See also *ibid.*, vol. IX, p. 181.

כלל גדול בתורה

The Dynamics of *Ahavat Yisrael*

The Dynamics of *Ahavat Yisrael*

Table of Contents

Introduction: Comprehensive Principles 21

Part One: The Halachic Perspective

I	Definition of the Precept	23
II	Qualification of the Precept	26
III	*Hoche'ach Tochi'ach*	30
IV	Sinners and Saints	33
V	Sin vs. Sinner	37
VI	Concern for the Erring	41
VII	"Children of G-d"	45

Part Two: The Philosophical Perspective

VIII	Unity of G-d and Israel	49
IX	One Body and One Soul	54
X	Gateway to G-d	58
XI	Universal Love	61
XII	Limbs of the *Shechinah*	64
XIII	"What is Hateful to You.."	68
XIV	Soul vs. Body	74

Conclusion: Prerequisite to Redemption 77

כלל גדול בתורה

The Dynamics of *Ahavat Yisrael*

Introduction
Comprehensive Principles

"Six-hundred-and-thirteen precepts were given to Moses.. David came and based them on eleven.. Michah came and based them on three.. Isaiah came and based them on two.. Habakuk came and based them on one.."[1]

The simple meaning of this passage is that there are certain principles in the Torah, the observance of which is conducive to a maximum observance of all the precepts, of the whole Torah. A sincere and consistent concentration on the eleven, six, three, two, or one, principles mentioned in

---

1. *Makot* 24a.

the passage quoted, must move man to a fulfillment of all the 613 precepts, because the latter are intimately intertwined with the former.[2]

It is in this sense, too, that we understand the well-known dictum: "'You shall love your fellow-man like yourself' (Leviticus 19:18) — R. Akiba said, This is a great rule of the Torah!"[3] In other words, the *mitzvah* of *Ahavat Yisrael* (love of a fellow-Jew) is one of the all-comprehensive principles of the Torah, the proper observance of which implies the observance and fulfillment of the other *mitzvot*.[4]

The concept of *Ahavat Yisrael* plays a dominant role in the teachings of Chassidism.[5] It is one of the major premises upon which Chassidism places special emphasis, and, in line with the above, bases the Torah-life and practices upon it. Chassidism offers elaborate expositions and original insights to this *mitzvah*, some of which we shall examine in context of its general perspective and implications.

---

2. See *Tanya*, ch. 33.
3. *Sifra* on Leviticus 19:18; *Yerushalmi, Nedarim* 9:4; *Bereishit Rabba*, end of ch. 24 (see *Minchat Yehudah ad loc.*).
4. See *Sefer Hachinuch*, no. 243; R. Judah Loew (Maharal), *Netivot Olam*, Ahavat Re'a, ch. 1; R. Dov Ber of Lubavitch, *Torat Chayim*, vol. I, Noach, ch. 33. *Cf.* below, sect. XIII-XIV.
5. See below, note 174.

Part One: The Halachic Perspective

I

Definition of the Precept

The precept of *Ahavat Yisrael* consists of two explicit *mitzvot*, one a commandment and one a prohibition:[6]

a. "You shall love your fellow-man like yourself."[7]
b. "You shall not hate your brother in your heart."[8]

Maimonides defines these in his *Sefer Hamitzvot* as follows:

---

6. *Cf.* R. Yerucham Fishel Perla's commentary on *Sefer Hamitzvot* of R. Saadia Gaon, I:19. This erudite and incisive commentary is a significant source for detailed discussions of most of the Halachic principles and issues touched upon in the first half of this study.
7. Leviticus 19:18.
8. Leviticus 19:17.

a. "..He commanded us to love one another even as we love ourselves, and that my compassion and love for my brother[-man] be as my compassion and love for myself with respect to his money, his person, and to whatever he possesses or desires. Whatever I wish for myself, I am to wish likewise for him; and whatever is hateful unto me or to whoever is attached to me, is likewise hateful unto me with respect to him. This is the meaning of His blessed saying, 'And you shall love your fellow like yourself.'"[9]

b. "..We are forbidden to hate one another, as stated in His saying, 'You shall not hate your brother in your heart.' *Sifra*[10] comments that this refers only to [the personal feeling of] enmity in the heart. When, however, manifesting this hatred and informing him about it, one does not violate this prohibition, though one would [still] violate 'You shall not revenge or carry a grudge,'[11] as well as the commandment, 'You shall love your fellow like yourself.' To harbour hatred in the heart, however, is the most grievous sin of all."[12]

Nachmanides[13] comments on the *mitzvah* of *Ahavat Yisrael*:

"The human heart cannot take upon itself to love

---

9. *Sefer Hamitzvot* I:206.
10. *Sifra* on Leviticus. 19:17. *Cf. Eliyahu Rabba* ch. 18, and below, notes 17, 19, 27 and 41.
11. Leviticus 19:18.
12. *Sefer Hamitzvot* II:302. *Cf. Sifre*, Shoftim, par. 187.
13. Commentary on Leviticus 19:17-18.

another with the same love as one has for oneself. Moreover, R. Akiba ruled already that, 'Your life takes precedence over that of your fellow-being.'[14] The Torah, however, commanded that one is to love another in every respect as one loves oneself with regards to all good .. to equate the love of both in his mind .. [as opposed to] desiring in his heart to be better off than his fellow. Scripture thus commands that such degrading jealousy should not exist in his heart, but that with regards to abundance of good one is to love his fellow in the same manner as one would act for oneself and not to set restrictions to love.."

Nachmanides thus appears to imply that the essence of this precept lies in an *active* furtherance of another's welfare and well-being, in terms of concrete and maximum actions, as opposed to a mere sentiment of the heart.[15]

---

14. *Baba Metzia* 62a. *Cf. Tanya,* Igeret Hakodesh, sect. 16.
15. See Maimonides, *Hilchot De'ot* 6:3, and *Hilchot Evel* 14:1.

II

Qualification of the Precept

The general ruling is that "it is incumbent upon every person to love each and everyone of Israel as himself," and that "whoever hates in his heart anyone of Israel transgresses a prohibition."[16] Nonetheless, Maimonides qualifies this in his Code:

> "'You shall love your fellow like yourself' means that what you would have others do unto you, do unto him *who is your brother in Torah and mitzvot*. For *re'acha* (your fellow-man) means 'he who is your equal in Torah and *mitzvot*.'"[17]

This qualification reflects the following teaching:

---

16. *Hilchot De'ot*, ch. 6.
17. *Hilchot Evel* 14:1.

"Man should not adopt a rule of 'Love the sages and hate the *am ha'aretz.*' His rule should be, 'Love them all, and hate only heretics, apostates, those leading astray, and informers.' Thus said David, 'Do not I hate them that hate You, G-d.'[18] But does not Scripture declare, 'You shall love your fellow like yourself, I am G-d;' and why, because 'I [G-d] created him!' However, if he acts as 'your people'[19] should act, then you must love him; if not, you must not love him."[20]

R. Nachman bar Yitzchak thus stated that in the case of a sinner it is not only permitted but a religious obligation to hate him, as it is said, "Fear of G-d is to hate evil" (Proverbs 8:13).[21] R. Nachman's statement is adopted as Halachic ruling, as recorded by Maimonides:

"The 'enemy' mentioned in the Torah [Exodus 23:5] does not refer to an alien enemy, but to an Israelite one. How can an Israelite have an Israelite enemy when Scripture says, 'You shall not hate your brother in your heart'? The sages decreed that if someone by himself[22] sees another committing a transgression and warns him against it, yet he will not desist, it is

---

18. Psalms 139:21f.
19. See *Baba Metzia* 48b on Exodus 22:27 (*cf. Meiri* on *Avot* 2:15).
20. *Avot deR. Nathan*, end of ch. 16. *Cf. Shabbat* 116a; *Pesachim* 113b; *Menorat Hama'or*, ed. Enelow, IV:p. 304. See below, sect. V-VI.
21. *Pesachim* 113b. *Cf. Ta'anit* 4b.
22. In that case the witness alone is to hate the sinner. If the sin was a public violation, i.e., there were two or more witnesses, it is incumbent upon all to hate him. See *Pesachim, ad loc.*

incumbent upon [the witness] to hate him until he will repent and leave his evil ways."[23]

Sefer Hachinuch cites the same ruling in different wording:

"Hatred of the wicked does not involve any prohibition. Indeed, one is obligated to hate them after oftentimes admonishing them for their sins and their refusal to repent, as it is written, 'Do not I hate them that hate You, G-d.' "[24]

A careful reading of these sources reveals some significant points. The permission and duty to hate the wicked is (a) contingent upon the prior fulfillment — by the witness(es) — of the commandment "You shall repeatedly rebuke your fellow-man;"[25] and (b) is limited to the duration of the sinner's rebellion. In other words, first one must admonish and rebuke the transgressor and do all that is possible to restore him to the right path. Only after one has duly and exhaustively observed this *mitzvah* according to all of its delineated rules,[26] and still finds the sinner persisting in

---

23. *Hilchot Rotze'ach* 13:14. *Shulchan Aruch*, Choshen Mishpat 272:11.
24. *Sefer Hachinuch*, no. 238. As for the comment of *Minchat Chinuch, ad loc.*, see *Sefer Hashlamah al Minchat Chinuch*, p. 92b.
25. Leviticus 19:17.
26. See *Zohar* III:85bf. *Hilchot De'ot* 6:6-9, and the references cited in *Sefer Hamada*, ed. Y. Cohen, Jerusalem 1964, and in *Marei Mekomot-Mishneh Torah* (Kehot: New York 1984), *Hilchot De'ot ad loc.* See also *Sefer Chassidim*, sect. 5-6, 39, and 413,

his rebellious ways, then one may (or must) express the hatred spoken of above.

---

and the commentaries *Berit Olam* and *Mekor Chessed; Shulchan Aruch*, Orach Chayim, sect. 608, and comm. *ad loc.*, and in *Shulchan Aruch Harav*, sect. 156:7-8; R. Isaiah Horowitz, *Shaloh*, Introduction; R. Chayim Medini, *Sedei Chemed*, Assifat Dinim, *s.v.* Hey: sect. 2 (ed. Kehot, vol. V:pp. 1951-6); R. Menachem Trivash, *Orach Mesharim*, sect. 31; R. Jonathan Steif, *Mitzvot Hashem* II:8, p. *59ff.*

III

Hoche'ach Tochi'ach

With respect to the *mitzvah* of *hoche'ach tochi'ach* (rebuking the sinner) there are several qualifications. For one thing, just as the precept of love is said to relate to *re'acha* as defined above, so, too, the precept of admonition is related to *amitecha*, i.e., one who is "with you in Torah and *mitzvot*."[27] Secondly, we are confronted by the following *Beraita*:

> "R. Tarfon said, I wonder whether there is anyone in this generation who is able to reprove; for if anyone

---

27. *Shulchan Aruch Harav*, Orach Chayim 156:6, and marginal note there. See *Eliyahu Rabba*, ch. 18 (ed. Friedmann, p. 109); *Keter Shem Tov*, sect. 280; *Tanya*, ch. 32 (cited below, sect. V). Cf. *Baba Metzia* 59a; *Shevu'ot* 30a; and the sources cited by R. Menachem Mendel of Lubavitch (Tzemach Tzedek) in *Sefer Kitzurim Vehe'arot*, p. 36.

says to [a sinner] 'remove the mote from between your eyes,' he would answer, 'remove the beam from between *your* eyes.' R. Eleazar ben Azarya said, I wonder whether there is anyone in this generation who is able to accept reproofs. R. Akiba said, I wonder whether there is anyone in this generation who knows how to reprove."[28]

Malbim[29] already noted that from this source it follows that there are three principles involved in the proper fulfillment of this *mitzvah*: (1) the suitability of the admonisher, i.e., that he himself be free of sin (R. Tarfon); (2) the suitability of the admonished to accept the reproof (R. Eleazar ben Azarya); and (3) the ability of the admonisher to reprove according to all legal aspects of this *mitzvah* (R. Akiba).

No less significant is another practical implication in this *Beraita*. In the days of the Tannaim it was questioned whether — on account of these three conditions — the *mitzvah* of *hoche'ach tochi'ach* could be fulfilled properly with all the legal consequences thereof.[30] In the sequel to this *Beraita*, R. Yochanan ben Nuri offers what appears to be clearly an exception to the rule:

"I call heaven and earth to witness for myself, that on

---

28. *Arachin* 16b; *Sifra*, Kedoshim: 9; and *Sifre*, Devarim, par. 1 — emended according to *Yalkut Shimoni*, Devarim par. 789, and *Dikdukei Soferim*.
29. *Hatorah Vehamitzvah* on *Sifra, ad loc.*, par. 43. Cf. commentary of R. Dov Ber of Mezhirech on *Tamid* 28a (*Or Torah*, ed. Kehot, sect. 486; *Likutim Yekarim*, sect. 117).
30. See *Mitzvot Hashem, op. cit.*, p. 63f. Cf. also *Netivot Olam*, Tochacha, ch. 3.

my account R. Akiba was reproved more than four or five times before Rabban Gamliel .. Yet notwithstanding that fact, I know of him that for every time his love for me increased, verifying that which has been said,[31] 'Do not reprove a scorner lest he hate you; reprove a wise man, and he will love you.'"

If this was the case in those days, the days of those aforetimes "who were like angels," how much more so in our own time when compared to them "we are as donkeys, and not even like the donkey of R. Pinchas ben Yair!"[32]

---

31. Proverbs 9:8.
32. *Yerushalmi, Shekalim* 5:1. Cf. *Shabbat* 112b; *Eruvin* 53a; *Yoma* 9b; *Zohar* III:2a.

IV

Sinners and Saints

Moreover, even if and when the sinner falls into the category of those that are to be hated (the 'enemy'), the community of Israel remains bound to him with obligations:

> "Even if he has not yet repented, and one finds him in difficulties with his burden, one must help him load or unload, and not leave him possibly to die. For the 'enemy' might tarry because of his property and meet with danger, and the Torah is very solicitous for the lives of Israelites — *whether of the wicked or the righteous*. Thus it is said,[33] 'Say unto them, as I live, says G-d, I have no pleasure in the death of the wicked, but that the wicked turn from his way and live.'"[34]

---

33. Ezekiel 33:11.
34. See references in note 23.

In fact, "if one encounters two people .. one an 'enemy' and the other a friend, one is obligated to load *for the 'enemy' first*, in order to subdue *yitzro* (his evil impulse)!"[35] Some commentators interpret *yitzro* to refer to the impulse of the sinner: the demonstration of the Torah's concern for the sinner will move him to subdue his impulse and repent of his evil ways. There is ample evidence, however, to interpret the term *yitzro* to refer no less to the benefactor: the one who wishes to fulfill the *mitzvah* of assisting another in need must guard against personalizing even legitimate hatred.[36]

In other words, even in the case of permissible, and possibly obligatory, hatred of the wicked (the 'enemy'), one must guard against personal involvement, against a *personal* hatred of the wicked *person*, as opposed to a hatred of the evil and sin in him. It is not the person *qua* person who is subject to hate, but the element and state of wickedness. This hate must remain impersonal. When it comes to rendering assistance, therefore, one is to look at the person *qua* human being, rather than his evil. The only way that this can be manifested is by the actual example of helping the 'enemy' first, before one's pious friend, thus suppressing the evil impulse of disregarding a fellow-human.

This consideration for the wicked is not merely in terms of assisting him in times of possible danger, and as a means toward a superior end (i.e., his ultimate *teshuvah*). R. Meir ben Todros Halevi notes that the Talmud itself reasons the

---

35. See *Baba Metzia* 32b, and *Tossafot* on *Pesachim* 113b, *s.v.* vera'a bo (vs. *Tossafot* on *Baba Metzia* 32b). Note commentaries on *Shulchan Aruch*, Choshen Mishpat 272:10, gloss of *Rema*.
36. See *Torah Shelemah* on Mishpatim 23:4, par. 47-48, and the notes *ad loc*. *Cf*. also *ibid*., Milu'im, ch. 10, p. 202*ff*.

principle of *beror lo mita yafah* (find the easiest form of execution for one who has committed a capital offense) on the basis of the Scriptural precept of "You shall love your fellow like yourself."[37] Thus even a sinner so corrupt that he deserves capital punishment, and thus surely rebuked and forewarned, remains within the category of one who must be loved like yourself![38]

---

37. *Yad Ramah* on *Sanhedrin* 52b. See *Shita Mekubetzet* on *Ketuvot* 37b.
38. One obvious exception is to be found in the case of the *meisit umadiach*. Of him it is written, "You shall not *toveh* unto him" (Deuteronomy 13:9). The word *toveh* is identified with *tohav*, and interpreted as loving or showing affection. *Sifre* on this verse thus deduces: on the basis of the all-encompassing *mitzvah* of "You shall love your fellow like yourself" we might think that we are commanded to love also him who leads others astray. Scripture therefore states *lo toveh* — you are not permitted to love him at all. This is then an explicit prohibition of the Torah which constitutes one of the 613 *mitzvot* (*Sefer Hamitzvot* II:17; *Hilchot Avodah Zara* 5:4).

Moreover, the one who has been led astray is prohibited from relaxing his hatred of the *meisit*: he must hate him, and if he relaxes his hatred he violates another negative precept, namely, "You shall not hearken unto him" (Deuteronomy 13:9). Whereas Scripture states "You shall surely help him" (Exodus 23:5) — which, as we have seen, includes the Israelite enemy, i.e., the wicked in general — we might think that we must assist the *meisit* as well; Scripture therefore states, "You shall not hearken unto him" (*Sefer Hamitzvot* II:18).

In addition to these prohibitions, there are three more: (1) The one led astray is forbidden to save the life of the *meisit* when finding him in danger. Though the general rule is "You shall not stand idly by the blood of your fellow" (Leviticus 19:16), of the *meisit* it is said "Your eye shall not pity him" (Deuteronomy 13:9). (2) The one led astray is forbidden to plead for the *meisit* to exculpate him. Even if he knows some argument in his favour, he is not to suggest it to him or to advance it himself. (3) The one led astray is forbidden to suppress anything known to him that is unfavourable to the *meisit* and may help bring punishment upon him, as it is written "You shall not conceal him" (*ibid.*); i.e., if you know anything unfavourable to him, you are not permitted to withhold that information. (*Sefer Hamitzvot* II:19-21; *Hilchot Avodah Zara*, ch. 5)

It may be argued that these five prohibitions relate only to the person that has been led astray by the *meisit*, as in each case it is said "the one led astray is forbidden.." Anyone else, then, would not be violating these Biblical injunctions, though well the principle of R. Nachman bar Yitzchak, which is derived *midivrei kabalah. Minchat Chinuch*, quoting *Mishnat Chachamim*, already raised this issue and left it unresolved (see *Minchat Chinuch*, sect. 458). Offhand, though, in view of *Sanhedrin* 29a etc. (ruled by Maimonides, *Hilchot Sanhedrin* 11:5) it would seem that the injunctions relate to others as well.

In any case, the very fact that the Torah distinguishes between the *meisit umadiach* and all other sinners, to the point that, as taught by *Sifre*, were it not for these explicit Biblical qualifications we would be applying the principles of *Ahavat Yisrael, azov ta'azov* etc., suggests of itself that those principles *do apply to other sinners!*

V

Sin *vs.* Sinner

In Maimonides, though, we find a distinction between two types of wicked:

> "When all these principles [of the faith] are kept by man, and his belief in them is sincere, he enters into *klal Yisrael* (community of Israel) and it is incumbent to love him and to care for him with all that G-d commanded us to do for one another by way of love and brotherhood. This applies even though he may have committed whatever transgressions possible by reason of his passion or the mastery of his evil inclination. [In the latter case] he shall be punished commensurate to his perversion, but he retains a share [in the world to come] notwithstanding the fact that he be of the *poshei Yisrael* (renegades of Israel). But he who doubts any one of these principles has left the *klal*, denied the very substance [of Judaism], and he is

called a *min*, *apikores* and *kotzetz binetiyot* — and it is obligatory to hate and destroy him. Of him it is said, 'Shall I not hate them that hate You, G-d'.."[39]

Maimonides thus differentiates between a *kofer be'ikar* and those who sin by reason of succumbing to their passions and desires: the former must be despised, while the latter is to be loved. This suggests a discrepancy with Maimonides' earlier cited rulings in the Code. The apparent inconsistency was noted already by R. Meir Arik.[40] He offers two suggestions to reconcile the passages, the first along the lines of our earlier reference to the *mitzvah* of *hoche'ach tochi'ach*, i.e., that the sinner to be loved may be in a status prior to having been rebuked. In conclusion he resolves the difficulty by reference to the celebrated chapter 32 in *Tanya*, where it is said:

".. As for the Talmudic statement to the effect that he who sees his fellow sinning should hate him and tell his master to hate him also, this applies to a companion in Torah and *mitzvot*, having already applied to him the precept of 'You shall repeatedly rebuke *amitecha*' — i.e., he who is 'with you in Torah and *mitzvot*' and who nevertheless has not repented of his sins, as stated in *Sefer Charedim*.[41]

But as for the person who is not one's peer, and is not on intimate terms with him, Hillel said, 'Be of the

---

39. Commentary on *Mishnah*, *Sanhedrin* 10:1 (ed. Kapach, p. 216f.). Cf. above, note 20.
40. See his glosses on *Minchat Chinuch*, sect. 238, in *Sefer Hashlama*, op. cit., p. 76b.
41. *Sefer Charedim*, Mitzvot Assey .. hatluyot balev I:24.

disciples of Aaron, loving peace and pursuing peace, loving the *creatures* and drawing them near to Torah.'[42] This means, that even in the case of those who are removed from G-d's Torah and His service, and therefore are classified as mere *creatures*, one must attract them with strong cords of love perchance one will succeed in drawing them near to the Torah and Divine service. Even if one were to fail, one has not forfeited the merit of the *mitzvah* of neighbourly love.

Even with regard to those who are close to him, and whom he has rebuked, yet they had not repented of their sins, *when enjoined to hate them there still remains the duty to love them also*, and both are true: *hatred* on account of the *wickedness* in them, and *love* on account of the aspect of the *hidden good in them* which is the Divine spark in them that animates their Divine soul. One should also arouse pity in his heart for [that Divine soul],[43] for it is held captive, as it were, in the evil of the *sitra achara* which triumphs over it in the wicked. Compassion destroys hatred and awakens love, as known from the text, 'To the House of Jacob who redeemed Abraham.'[44]

(As for King David, peace unto him, who said, 'I hate them with a consuming hatred,'[45] he referred but to

---

42. *Avot* 1:12.
43. See *Tanya*, ch. 45.
44. Isaiah 29:22. *Cf. Vayikra Rabba* 36:4. See R. Dov Ber of Mezhirech, *Or Torah*, sect. 360, and *Likutei Amarim*, sect. 99; R. Shneur Zalman of Liadi, *Torah Or*, Shemot: p. 51b.
45. Psalms 139:22.

minim and *apikorsim* (apostates and heretics) who have no portion in the G-d of Israel, as stated in the *Gemara*, tractate *Shabbat*, beginning of chapter 16.)"

VI

Concern for the Erring

The concepts of *kofer be'ikar* and *apikores* who are to be hated beg for further clarification. Various authorities point out that there is a distinct difference between a deliberate denial of accepted doctrine and a mistaken interpretation. According to this distinction, pointed out in detail by R. Shimon ben Zemach Duran,[46] he who denies even the most minute detail of the Torah while *knowing it to be an authoritative teaching* of Torah and Jewish tradition is a heretic.[47] But he who in principle affirms and accepts the teachings of our tradition, but in sincere reflection is misled

---

46. Introduction to his commentary on Job, and his *Magen Avot* 8:9.
47. See *Sanhedrin* 99a; Maimonides, Commentary on *Mishnah*, Intr. to *Sanhedrin* X, principle 8, and *Hilchot Teshuvah* 3:8.

to differ in details from the accepted truth, is merely in error and not a heretic.

R. Joseph Albo elaborates on this theme in his introduction to, and discussion of, the concept of principles of faith in Judaism.[48] He quotes the well-known case of R. Hillel who identified King Hezekiah with the intended Messiah and concluded that there shall be no Mashiach for Israel because they already enjoyed him in the days of Hezekiah.[49] After rejecting various explanations for this strange passage, R. Joseph Albo concludes that obviously R. Hillel erred and was guilty of a sin[50] for not believing that the Messianic redemption to come will still be through the agency of a descendant of King David. Yet R. Hillel could not possibly be regarded as a heretic, as evident from the Talmud which continues to quote him authoritatively.[51] R. David ibn Abi Zimra, too, refers to this Talmudic passage, arrives at the same conclusion, and explains: As R. Hillel's denial was based on his sincere conviction that his opinion reflects the true meaning of the relevant prooftexts, he was an *annus* and thus *patur*.[52]

In other words, a case of honest and sincere misunderstanding and intellectual error is not to be regarded as one of *kefirah*. How much less so, then, can we speak of the legal implications of *kefirah* in the case of those misguided by

---

48. *Ikkarim* I:ch. 1-2.
49. *Sanhedrin* 99a. Cf. ibid. 98b.
50. See *ibid.*: "R. Joseph said, 'May G-d forgive him!'"
51. Note also R. Joseph Albo's reference, *ad loc.*, to Rabad's stricture on *Hilchot Teshuvah* 3:7.
52. Responsa of *Radvaz* IV:187. Cf. R. Yosef Yitzchak of Lubavitch, *Sefer Hamaamarim* 5711, p. 242a.

their parents and teachers, those raised and trained in heterodox environments, who are truly

> "*like children taken captives by them and raised in their [false] religion, whose status is that of an* annus *.. Therefore, efforts must be made to bring them back in repentance, to draw them near by friendly relations, so that they may return to the strength-giving source, namely the Torah!*"[53]

The efforts for those astray include also a religious obligation to pray for sinners that they return to the fold.[54] For it is *sin* that we must detest, and not the sinners. Thus it is written,[55] "*Yitamu chata'im* — let sins be consumed from the earth, and the wicked shall be no more; bless G-d, O my soul":

> "*Is it written* 'Let chotim (*sinners*) *be consumed?*' *It is written* 'chata'im (*sins*)'! *Also, look at the conclusion of the verse:* 'And the resha'im (*wicked*) *shall be no more.*' *For when* sins *shall be consumed there will be no more wicked people. Thus pray for them that they should repent, and there will be no more wicked!*"[56]

---

53. Maimonides, *Hilchot Mamrim* 3:3. Cf. also his Commentary on *Mishnah, Chulin* 1:2.
54. *Midrash Hane'elam, Zohar* I:105a, and see *Nitzutzei Orot*, and *Nitzutzei Zohar, ad loc. Sefer Chassidim*, sect. 76, and *Mekor Chessed ad loc.* Cf. *Sanhedrin* 37a, and the commentary of R. Isaiah Berlin, appended to his *Minei Targuma*, p. 35a; and below, sect. VII and XI, and note 130.
55. Psalms 104:35.
56. *Berachot* 10a, and see *Tossafot Harosh ad loc.*

R. Yehuda said: "'Yitamu chata'im' — *let the sinners become* temimim *(perfect; upright), and the wicked shall be no more, i.e., they will no longer be wicked. Only then can we truly say, 'Bless G-d, O my soul!'"*[57]

---

57. *Midrash Tehilim* 104:27.

VII

"Children of G-d"

In consideration of this definition, in addition to the earlier observation that the *mitzvah* of *hoche'ach tochi'ach* can no longer be fulfilled fully and properly, we must conclude, as noted by a number of authorities,[58] that nowadays we no longer have the category of *apikores*.

Thus the precept of "Love your fellow like yourself" and the principle of R. Nachman bar Yitzchak to hate the wicked are not mutually exclusive. To hate the wicked does not exclude a simultaneous love for them. The implicit

---

58. See *Sefer Hamaamarim 5711, op. cit.*, p. 242a. *Chazon Ish* on *Hilchot De'ot* VI, and on *Yoreh De'ah* 13:16; *Encyclopaedia Talmudit*, s.v. apikores. Note also the interesting definition of *apikores* in R. Nachman of Bratzlav, *Likutei Moharan*, part I, 64:2; and in R. Eliyahu Dessler, *Michtav Me'eliyahu*, vol. I, p. 173f.

difference between hating evil and personalizing that hatred can be seen reflected in practical legal rulings. For example,[59] a judge is disqualified when personally involved with those appearing before him, as in a case of personal friendship or personal hatred. He would not be disqualified, however, when following the principle of R. Nachman bar Yitzchak, i.e., hating the sin or evil committed by those before his court without having translated that to personal enmity. This, indeed, follows clearly from the very proof-text referred to by R. Nachman: "Fear of G-d is to hate *evil*."

Sinners are an integral part of the body of Israel, whether we speak of the body of the nation as a whole or the body of every individual.[60] Of all of Israel it is said, "You are children of G-d."[61] To be sure, R. Yehuda was of the opinion that this verse applies only when we behave as becoming to children; but when we do not behave as G-d's children then we lose that designation. R. Meir, on the other hand, states that "either way you are designated 'children,' as it is said,[62] 'They are sottish children,' and[63] 'They are children in whom is no faith,' 'A seed of evil-doers, children that deal corruptly,'[64] as well as[65] 'It shall come to pass that in the place where it was said unto them, You are not My people, it shall be said unto them, You are the children of the living G-d.'"[66] In disputes between R. Meir and R. Yehuda

---

59. See *Pitchei Teshuvah*, and R. Jonathan Eybeshitz's *Tumim* (note 9), on *Choshen Mishpat* 7:7.
60. See below, sect. IX-XII.
61. Deuteronomy 14:1.
62. Jeremiah 4:22.
63. Deuteronomy 32:2.
64. Isaiah 1:4.
65. Hosea 2:1.
66. *Kidushin* 36a; *Sifre* on Deuteronomy 14:1.

THE DYNAMICS OF AHAVAT YISRAEL 47

the Halachah generally follows R. Yehuda.[67] In this case, however, we rule as R. Meir who adduced Scriptural proofs to support his view.[68]

Moreover, there is the axiomatic premise that a Jew is forever designated by the term "Israel" — implying a permanence of the intrinsic holiness attached to the people of Israel — even when he is a sinner.[69] "Even the emptiest among you are full of *mitzvot* like a pomegranate [is full of seeds],"[70] and they are beloved unto G-d "like Jacob and his sons."[71]

To be sure, there are and remain basic differences in our relationships to sinners and to saints. They are clearly not the same, as already implied in the Scriptural precept of "Love *re'acha* [your peer in Torah and *mitzvot*] like yourself." The comprehensive principle of *Ahavat Yisrael* thus entails two separate aspects: (1) The Biblical, legal obligation of "Love *re'acha* like yourself," which is subject to gradations and variations; and (2) an absolute and unqualified obligation by virtue of the very nature of a fellow-Jew. As the second aspect relates to the very essence of the Jew ("children of

---

67. *Eruvin* 46b. See *Yad Malachi*, I: *s.v.* reish, par. 581-2.
68. Responsa of *Rashba*, I:194 and 242; Chida, *Midbar Kedemot*, *s.v.* bet, nos. 2 and 4; *s.v.* kaf, no. 5; and *s.v.* mem, no. 11. See *Baba Batra* 10a, and Maharsha *ad loc.*, s.v. amar ley; *Bamidbar Rabba* 2:15. *Cf. Likutei Sichot*, vol. XI, p. 3. See also R. Sholom Dov Ber of Lubavitch, *Besha'ah Shehikdimu-5672*, vol. I:pp. 56 and 121.
69. *Sanhedrin* 44a, and Rashi *ad loc.* See *Kuzary* I:95. *Cf. Einayim Lamishpat, ad loc.*
70. *Berachot* 57a. The version in *Eruvin* 19a and *Chagigah* 27a, is "even the *poshim* (rebels; willful transgressors — see *Yoma* 36b) among you.."
71. Rashi on Shir Hashirim 4:1.

G-d;" a "portion of G-d from Above"), it does not allow for variations and extends to the wicked as well as to the righteous.[72]

---

72. See *Sefer Ha'arachim-Chabad*, vol. I, *s.v.* Ahavat Yisrael, p. 616*ff.* (and the notes *ad loc.*) on this distinction and its implications.

Part Two:
The Philosophical Perspective

VIII
Unity of G-d and Israel

The philosophical aspect of *Ahavat Yisrael* entails two intricately interwoven considerations: (a) the bond of the G-d-Israel relationship, and (b) the bond of the interrelationship between the members of the people of Israel.

The special bond between G-d and His chosen people Israel is mentioned explicitly and implicitly in numerous verses of our sacred Scriptures as well as in a multitude of passages in the Talmud and Midrashim, with wide elucidation in the post-Talmudic writings. It will suffice to touch upon a few basic, and comprehensively representative quotations.

The very beginning of the Torah enunciates the special character of Israel: "*Bereishit bara Elokim* — In the beginning G-d created..." The word *reishit* is a term designating, and referring to, the people of Israel. *Bereishit* thus means, "For the sake of (or: because of) Israel, G-d created the heaven and the earth."[73] For it is through Israel, endowed with the Torah and observing the precepts of the Torah (which is the underlying 'blueprint' and foundation for the creation[74]) that the purpose of the universe becomes realized.[75] The thought of Israel preceded all: G-d thought of Israel before the creation,[76] and it is the rock upon which the world was founded.[77]

This principle, typifying the character and mission of Israel, can be taken as an introduction and explanation to "You are a nation consecrated unto G-d, your G-d. G-d has

---

73. *Vayikra Rabba* 36:4; *Tanchuma*, ed. Buber, Bereishit, par. 3 and 10; Rashi on Genesis 1:1. See *Eliyahu Rabba*, ch. 14, and the comment thereon in R. Shmuel of Lubavitch, *Mayim Rabim-5636*, ch. 175.

    Note that the 22 letters of the Hebrew alphabet divide into five groupings, each having its own organ of articulation (larynx; palate; tongue; teeth; and lips); *Sefer Yetzirah* 2:3; *Zohar* III:227bf., and the sources cited there in *Nitzutzei Zohar*. Following the principle that the letters in any one group (thus having the same organ of articulation) are interchangeable (see Rashi on Leviticus 19:16), the *tav* can be substituted by the *lamed*. This means that the word *reishit* is composed of the same letters as the term *Yisrael*!

74. See *Bereshit Rabba* 1:1 and 6; *Tanchuma*, Bereishit:1; *Zohar* I:5a.

75. See *Avodah Zara* 3a; *Tanchuma*, Bereishit:1; Rashi on Genesis 1:31.

76. *Bereishit Rabba* 1:4; *Zohar* I:24a.

77. *Yalkut Shimoni*, Balak, par. 766.

THE DYNAMICS OF AHAVAT YISRAEL

chosen you from all nations on the face of the earth to be unto Him a specially treasured nation."[78]

This bond between G-d and Israel is not some provisional covenant. Israel is to G-d more than a 'partner in a treaty': it is *am kerovo*[79] — a people that is His 'relative.'[80] G-d has with Israel a 'relationship of the flesh,' as it were, as it is written,[81] "To the *she'erit* of His heritage": *she'erit* is an idiom of *she'er basar* (relation of the flesh), a close relative. For that reason He senses, as it were, all that happens to Israel, as it is written, "In all their sorrows, He is afflicted."[82] Thus come what may, Israel remains the Divine heritage, with G-d saying: "What shall I do if I punish them, for the pain will be My own!"[83]

The most poignant expression of this relationship is to be found in the verse, "You are children of G-d, your G-d!"[84]

This bond, therefore, is uniquely close and innate, and it is as eternal as it is unique. While Israel is forever bound by its special obligation to abide by the will of G-d as expressed in the Torah, G-d, too, has avowed that He will "never

---

78. Deuteronomy 7:6 and 14:2. See also Exodus 19:5*f.* and Deuteronomy 26:18*f.*
79. Psalms 148:14.
80. *Midrash Tehilim* 4:4. See R. Shneur Zalman of Liadi, *Likutei Torah*, Re'ey, p. 19d.
81. Micha 7:18.
82. Isaiah 63:9. See *Mechilta (deR. Yishmael*, and *deRashby)*, *Tanchuma, Rabba,* and Rashi, on Exodus 3:2; *Mechilta* (both) on Exodus 12:41; *Zohar* I:120b, and III:219b. See also below, sect. XII.
83. *Tomer Devorah* 1:4.
84. See above, notes 66 and 68.

exchange them for another people, nor change or alter them for another nation, nor will He destroy them."[85]

In this context we can readily understand the Zoharic statement that the Holy One, blessed, be He, and Israel, are completely bound up one in the other.[86] Hence it follows also that love of G-d implies of necessity love of Israel, even as love of Israel must imply love of G-d.[87] This holds true in both the positive sense of love, as well as in the negative sense of hatred: whoever hates Israel, per force also hates Him who created the world.[88]

The Baal Shem Tov expressed this in a pithy statement:

"Love of Israel is love of G-d. 'You are children of G-d, your G-d;' he who loves the Father also loves the children!"[89]

He taught furthermore:

"The precept 'Love your fellow like yourself' is an interpretation and exposition of the precept 'Love

---

85. *Eliyahu Rabba*, end of ch. 24 (ed. Friedmann, p. 127); and *Eliyahu Zutta*, end of ch. 10; *Ruth Rabba*, Petichta: 3; *Gitin* 57b; Rashi on Deuteronomy 29:12. See also *Mayim Rabim-5636, op. cit.*, ch. 56-59 and 61, in comment on *Eliyahu Rabba*, ch. 6.
86. *Zohar* III:73a.
87. See *Pessikta Rabaty*, Ki Tissa, par. 11 (in ed. Friedmann, p. 39b). *Vayikra Rabba* 2:5. See below, note 89.
88. *Mechilta* on Exodus 15:7. *Sifre* on Numbers 10:35 (see Rashi on both these verses and on Numbers 31:3). *Sha'arei Kedushah* II:4, *s.v.* sinah. See below, sect. XI-XII.
89. *Keter Shem Tov*, Hossafot: par. 141. See *Netivot Olam*, Ahavat Re'a, ch. 1. See *Likutei Sichot*, vol. II, pp. 298, 300, and 499f.

G-d, your G-d.'[90] *He who loves an Israelite loves G-d. For every Israelite contains within himself a 'portion of G-d Above.'*[91] *Thus loving him, i.e., his inner self, is love of G-d.''*[92]

---

90. Deuteronomy 6:5.
91. *Tanya,* ch. 2. See *Sha'arei Kedushah* I:1; *Reishit Chochmah, Sha'ar Ha'ahavah,* ch. 3; R. Shabtay Sheftel Halevi, *Shefa Tal,* Introduction, and his *Nishmat Shabtay Halevi.*
92. *Keter Shem Tov,* Hossafot: par. 18. See *Likutei Sichot,* vol. II, pp. 298, 300, and esp. 499.

IX
"One Body and One Soul"

The intimate G-d-Israel relationship is one basic aspect of the precept of *Ahavat Yisrael*. Closely related to it is the other aspect, that of the inter-relationship within Israel itself.

This inter-relationship is best illustrated in the Midrashic comment on "You shall be unto Me a Kingdom of Priests and a Holy Nation"[93]: the singular tense of 'Holy Nation' teaches that all of Israel is as *one body and one soul*. As anyone of them sins, all are affected; as anyone of them is afflicted, all of them feel it.[94]

---

93. Exodus 19:6.
94. *Mechilta deRashby* on Exodus 19:6 (ed. Epstein-Melamed, p. 139). See also *Mechilta deR. Yishmael* on this verse; *Yerushalmi, Nedarim* 9:4, and *Korban Ha'edah*, and *Pnei Mosheh ad loc.*; *Radvaz* on *Hilchot Mamrim* 2:4; *Reishit Chochmah, ad loc.*; *Shaloh*, Sha'ar Ha'otiot: bet, *s.v.* beriyot.

R. Shimon bar Yochai compares this to a group of people cruising on a boat, and one of them boring a hole beneath his own place. His fellow-travelers cry out: "What are you doing?" Said he to them: "What does that matter to you? I am boring under my own place!" Said they: "Because the water will come up and flood the boat for all of us!"[95]

The innate unity and interrelationship of Israel is itself rooted in the G-d-Israel relationship. Their common origin in G-d relates the members of Israel to one another: "They are truly like brothers, as it is said, 'You are the children of G-d, your God.' "[96] Likewise it is said, "Have we not all one Father? Has not one G-d created us? Why do we deal treacherously, every man against his brother, profaning the covenant of our fathers?"[97] Thus even as one cannot speak of division in Divinity, all of Israel are a unit, a singular entity, mutually bound up one in the other.[98]

This concept is widely cited and expounded, especially in the writings of the mystics. Its implications are far-reaching and find expression in both the positive sense (the effects of the practice of *Ahavat Yisrael*) and the negative sense (the effects of the failure to practice *Ahavat Yisrael*).

R. Mosheh Cordovero (*Remak*) writes:

"All of Israel are related to one another because the

---

95. *Vayikra Rabba* 4:6. *Zohar* III:122a, and comment. *Mikdash Melech*, and *Nitzutzei Orot, ad loc.; Eliyahu Rabba,* ch. (11) 12 (ed. Friedmann, p. 56).
96. See Maimonides, *Hilchot Matnot Aniyim* 10:2. Cf. *Reishit Chochmah, ad loc.*
97. Malachi 2:10. See *Reishit Chochmah, ad loc.*
98. See *Tziyun Yerushalayim,* and *Korban Ha'edah,* on *Yerushalmi, Nedarim* 9:4.

souls compound one another: there is in this one part of the other, and in the other part of this one [thus each soul compounding all others]. That is why a multitude performing a *mitzvah* cannot be compared [with the few who do so]..[99]

"For this reason, also, all of Israel are surety one for the other,[100] because each one possesses literally a portion of his fellow.[101] Thus when one sins, he blemishes himself as well as the portion which the other possesses in him. It follows, then, that because of this shared portion, the other is a surety for him.

"All of them, therefore, are related to one another, and thus it is only right that one should seek the well-being of his fellow: to eye benevolently the well-being of his fellow, and that his honour be as dear to him as his own, for *he is he* [they are truly identical] in the most literal sense. That is why we are commanded 'Love your fellow as yourself.'"[102]

R. Isaac Luria (*Ari*) reiterated this interpretation, and

---

99. See *Sifra*, and Rashi, on Leviticus 26:8. Cf. *Bereshit Rabba* 68:7.

On the merits of a multitude joined together (*tzibur*) over individuals, see *Zohar* I:234a (also *ibid.*, 167b); *Berachot* 8a, and *Ta'anit* 8a. *Kuzary* III:19; R. Joseph Gikatilla, *Sha'arei Orah*, end of ch. 2. See also *Sefer Ha'arachim-Chabad, s.v.* Ahavat Yisrael, note 178.

100. *Shevu'ot* 39a.

101. See R. Dov Ber of Mezhirech, *Likutei Amarim*, sect. 177, and *Or Torah*, sect. 248, interpreting *areivim zeh bazeh* (surety one for the other) as *me'uravim zeh bazeh* (intermingled and intermeshed one with the other).

102. *Tomer Devorah* I:4.

thus explains the reason why he recited the full text of the liturgical confessions of sins notwithstanding the fact that it refers to transgressions he had never committed. He notes:

> "The sages instituted the plural form of '*we* have sinned..,' rather than '*I* have sinned..,' because all of Israel is one entity. Thus even if one did not commit a certain sin, he still ought to confess to it; because if another did transgress, it is just as if he himself had done so. Even when an individual prays and confesses at home, he should still recite the confession in plural form, because the sin of any one is as if *all* had sinned together by virtue of the surety between all souls."[103]

---

103. R. Chaim Vital, *Likutei Torah-Ta'amei Hamitzvot*, Kedoshim (on Leviticus. 19:18); idem, *Peri Eitz Chayim*, Sha'ar XII: ch. 8; *Shulchan Aruch Arizal*, Hilchot Bet Haknesset, par. 8. See also *Reishit Chochmah*, Sha'ar Hayirah, ch. 14. The Ari's words are elucidated in R. Menachem Mendel of Lubavitch (Tzemach Tzedek), *Derech Mitzvotecha*, s.v. Ahavat Yisrael, p. *55f.*

X
Gateway to G-d

The people of Israel may appear to be but an aggregate of separate entities, of different and distinct individuals. This seeming division and separation, however, is but a physical one — on account of the separate and distinct physical bodies. In truth, however, Israel is an essentially singular entity, united and bound together by its all-encompassing soul.[104]

---

104. See references above, note 94; and *Derech Mitzvotecha*, p. 56. *Reishit Chochmah*, Sha'ar Ha'anavah, ch. 5, notes that the interrelationship is based not only on spiritual grounds (i.e., with reference to the soul), but also on the physical level (with reference to the body). He quotes Malachi 2:10 as a proof text, and traces this idea to our common descent from the Patriarchs. He adds, moreover, that all of us share also a common archetype of the body, originally created and formed by G-d. See also *Yom Tov shel Rosh Hashanah-5666*, p. 603.

In this context, R. Isaac Luria prescribed that before one begins the daily prayer, "one is to undertake the acceptance of the *mitzvah* of 'Love your fellow like yourself,' with the intent to love every one of the people of Israel like his very own self. This way his prayer will ascend combined with all the prayers of Israel, able to ascend Heavenward and to be effective."[105]

The precept of *Ahavat Yisrael* is the very gate through which one can come to stand before G-d in prayer, and by merit of which the prayer will be received favourably.[106] Thus said the Baal Shem Tov: "*Ahavat Yisrael* is the first portal leading into the courtyards of G-d."[107]

R. Menachem Mendel of Lubavitch (*Tzemach Tzedek*) explained the *Ari's* words more elaborately: In order to attain the ultimate in prayer, the soul needs be complete and healthy. This means that the soul must be united with all the souls of Israel, just as the health of a bodily organ requires the health of all the veins it contains. To hate anyone of Israel implies to separate and exclude from one's own soul the part of that other. Hence there would be a mutilation and defect in one's own soul on account of that part (of the person hated) being lacking.

When one is blemished this way, one cannot ascend in favour before G-d, as it is written, "Whosoever has a defect shall not approach to offer..."[108] For the *En Soph*, compris-

---

105. *Sha'ar Hakavanot*, beginning; *Peri Eitz Chayim*, Sha'ar Hakorbonot, end of ch. 2 (Sha'ar Olam Ha'asiya, ch. 1); *Shulchan Aruch Arizal*, ibid., par. 1.
106. *Hayom Yom*, p. 67.
107. *Keter Shem Tov*, Hossafot, par. 139. Cf. *Midrash Tehilim* 118:17.
108. Leviticus 21:17.

ing them all, will not tolerate him because of that deficiency.[109]

And thus writes R. Shneur Zalman of Liadi (the *Alter Rebbe*) in one of his pastoral letters:[110]

"..'Be of humble spirit before every person'[111] in general.[112] For it is an established principle and truism that every one becomes better through his fellow-being.[113] Thus it is written, 'All the men of Israel.. as one man associated together,'[114] that is, just as one man is composed of many limbs; and when these become separated this affects the heart, 'for out of it flow the issues of life.'[115] With us, therefore, by all of us being as truly one person, the Divine service will be established in the heart, and from the affirmative [you may infer the negative]. That is why it is said, 'To serve Him as *one part*'.."[116]

---

109. *Derech Mitzvotecha*, s.v. Ahavat Yisrael. See also *Siddur im Dach* (Kehot 1965), p. 22b; *Likutei Sichot*, vol. I, p. 201, and vol. II, p. 597.
110. *Tanya*, Igeret Hakodesh, sect. 22-B.
111. *Avot* 4:10.
112. That is, literally 'before *any* individual,' even the 'most worthless' — see commentary of Maimonides on this *Mishnah*, and *Tanya*, beg. of ch. 30.
113. See *Zohar* I:234a, also *ibid*. 167b. *Kuzary* III:19. *Likutei Torah*, Nitzavim, p. 44a-b.
114. Judges 20:11. Cf. *Chagigah* 26a.
115. Proverbs 4:23. See *Igeret Hakodesh*, sect. 31 (cited below, section XII).
116. Zephaniah 3:9.

XI

Universal Love

The wholeness and completeness required to approach G-d thus means that the soul do not lack any part. The acknowledgment of an all-comprehensive association undertaken when avowing the *mitzvah* of *Ahavat Yisrael* implies an association with any and every Jew, without exception. *Ahavat Yisrael* is, and by definition *must* be, universal. It entails, as the Baal Shem Tov taught,[117] a dedicated and unconditional love even to such a Jew as one has never seen or heard about. Not a single Jew is expendable. The loss of any one individual is as the loss of a great multitude,[118] and

---

117. *Keter Shem Tov*, Hossafot, par. 140. See *Likutei Sichot*, vol. I, p. 201, and vol. II, p. 435. Note the explanation for this principle in *Likutei Sichot*, vol. XXI, p. 51.
118. *Mechilta*, and Rashi, on Exodus 19:21.

the lack of any one renders the whole community incomplete and deficient.[119]

"No cause whatsoever should prevent one from doing good to others. Not even sins or the misdeeds of unworthy persons should be considered when they would prevent one from doing good to those who need it! Just as G-d provides 'from the horned buffalo to the brood of the vermin,'[120] and does not despise any creature — (for if He were to despise creatures because of their insignificance, they could not exist even for one moment[121]) — but sets His Providence upon them, extending mercy to all, so, too, man must be benevolent to all, despising no creature. Even the most insignificant creature must assume importance in man's eyes and be subject to his concern...

"Man must train himself to do two things: first, to honour all creatures by recognizing in them the exalted nature of the Creator who in wisdom created man. The wisdom of the Creator is in all creatures. Thus one is to see for himself that they are exceedingly esteemed by virtue of the fact that the Creator of all, the most exalted Wise One, busied Himself with them by creating them. To despise them, Heaven forbid, is tantamount to touching the honour of their Creator!.. It is evil in the eyes of the Holy One, blessed be He, if any of His creatures are despised.. Thus man should see in them *chochmah* (the

---

119. *Mechilta* on Exodus 19:11. *Devarim Rabba* 7:9.
120. *Avodah Zara* 3b.
121. See *Pardes Rimonim* IV: end of ch. 10, and VI:8. *Tanya*, Sha'ar Hayichud, ch. 1, and Igeret Hakodesh, sect. 25.

Divine Wisdom; their Divine element),[122] and not a cause for them to be despised.

"Secondly, one must train oneself to induce in the heart a love for all people, *even the wicked*, as if they were his brothers and more so.. One is to love the wicked in his heart, saying, 'Would that these were righteous, returning in repentance, so that they would all be great and acceptable to the Omnipresent,'[123] as the faithful lover of all Israel[124] said,[125] 'Would that all the people of G-d were prophets'.."[126]

R. Dov Ber, the Maggid of Mezhirech, expressed this same idea by the terse and pithy statement that the *mitzvah* of *Ahavat Yisrael* demands that one love a wholly wicked person just like a wholly righteous person![127]

---

122. See *Mystical Concepts in Chassidism*, ch. III: sect. 4.
123. See above, notes 54-57.
124. See *Menachot* 65a.
125. Numbers 11:29.
126. *Tomer Devorah*, beg. and end of ch. II. Cf. *Meiri* on *Yoma* 75a; *Reishit Chochmah*, Sha'ar Ha'anavah, ch. 4-5. See also above, note 54.
127. *Or Torah*, Hossafot, par. 42. See *Likutei Sichot*, vol. II, p. 299f.

XII

"Limbs of the *Shechinah*"

The inter-relationship of Israel implies, then, that divisiveness mutilates and blemishes the wholeness of Israel in general, and of the individuals involved in particular. Moreover, it affects the G-d-Israel relationship as well. Just as one Jew is affected by another, so, too, as it were, G-d is 'affected' by Israel. G-d refers to Israel as *tamati*[128] — "which means, so to speak, 'My twin' .. Just as when one twin suffers pain in the head, the other feels it also, so, too, as it were, the Holy One, blessed be He, said,[129] 'I am with him in trouble.'"[130]

---

128. Song 5:2.
129. Psalms 91:15.
130. *Shemot Rabba* 2:5; *Shir Rabba* 5:2. See above, notes 82-83. Note that this Divine *pathos* relates to the sufferings of the wicked as well, as stated explicitly in the *Mishnah, Sanhedrin*

Thus just as our Father in Heaven rejoices, as it were, in the loving harmony and fellowship of His children below, the *Shechinah* is in a state of anguish and suffers, as it were, when there is a division of hearts and minds:

> "The *Shechinah* suffers in the *galut*,[131] as it were. It is, metaphorically speaking, like a bodily ailment.. Illness or health depend on the extension and flow of the life-force vested in the blood, which flows from the heart to all organs.[132] 'Turning about, turning about, goes the spirit of life'[133] and the blood into all the limbs, through the veins absorbed in them, and returns to the heart.
>
> "Now, when the circulation and flow of this spirit of life always functions properly, in the proper order arranged for it by the Fountainhead of Life, blessed be He, man is perfectly healthy. For all the limbs are bound together and receive their proper vitality from the heart through this circulation. If, however, there is anywhere some malfunction, restraining, hindering or reducing the circulation of the blood with the spirit of life vested in it, that bond which ties all limbs to the heart by means of the (blood-) circulation is broken or diminished. This will cause man to fall ill and sick, may G-d have mercy.

46a (also *Chagigah* 15a). *Cf.* the Baal Shem Tov's lament about the Frankists' apostasy, in *Shivchei Habesht*, ed. Mundshein, p. 157.
131. *Tikunei Zohar* 25:70b.
132. See above, note 115. *Cf. Zohar* III:221b, and *ibid.*, 225a and 232b; *Tikunei Zohar* 13:29a.
133. Ecclesiastes 1:6.

"Precisely so, metaphorically speaking, all the souls of Israel are regarded as the 'limbs' of the *Shechinah*[134] — which (Itself) is referred to as the 'heart,'[135] as it is written, 'the Rock of my heart.'[136] Thus it is also written, 'I shall *dwell* in their midst,'[137] for the term *Shechinah* denotes the Light of G-d dwelling throughout (all) worlds .. to infuse them with vitality. The flow of this life-force is by means of a prior investment in the souls of Israel.[138] For all things created .. are unable to receive (their Divine) vivification .. to become living and subsisting realities, except through the souls (of Israel) which rose in His thought and preceded the creation of the worlds..[139]

"In context of these words and truisms, which it is impossible to explain properly in writing, it follows that the *Shechinah* is referred to as 'heart' and the souls as 'limbs.' This teaches us that when all the souls are attached and bound together, the circulation and flow of the life-force and effluence 'turns about, turns about' .. to bind and join them all to 'G-d who is One,'[140] to be attached to Him, blessed be He..[141]

"Thus is understood the saying of our sages, of

---

134. *Zohar* III:17a, and *ibid.* 231b. *Tikunei Zohar* 21:52a.
135. *Tikunei Zohar* 13:29a; *ibid.* 21:49b and 52a.
136. Psalms 73:26. See *Shir Rabba* 5:2. *Zohar* I:59a, and II:128b.
137. Exodus 25:8.
138. See *Zohar* III:221b. *Kuzary* II:36.
139. See above, notes 76-77, and also *Bereishit Rabba* 8:3.
140. Deuteronomy 6:4. See Rashi *ad loc.*
141. *Cf. Netivot Olam*, Ahavat Re'a, ch. 3.

blessed memory,[142] that the destruction of the Second Temple and the Fall of Israel into exile, and the withdrawal of the *Shechinah* and Its descent to Edom, into a state of exile,[143] as it were — all this was caused by the sin of *sinat chinam* (gratuitous hatred) and a division of hearts, may the Merciful save us.[144] That is why (the *Shechinah*) is referred to as ailing, metaphorically speaking..."[145]

Any flaw in *Ahavat Yisrael* is thus seen to affect *Knesset Yisrael*, in both the colloquial and the essential senses of this term — i.e., the community of Israel literally, and its source, the *Shechinah* — and mutilates and blemishes the one whose observance of this *mitzvah* is defective.

---

142. *Yoma* 9b. *Cf. Netivot Olam*, Lev Tov, near the end.
143. See *Megilah* 29a (*Dikdukei Soferim, ad loc.*); *Mechilta* on Exodus 12:41; *Sifre* on Numbers 10:35 and 35:34. *Cf. Yerushalmi, Ta'anit* 1:1.
144. *Cf. Sifre*, and *Rabba*, on Numbers 6:26; *Bereishit Rabba* 38:6; *Avot deR. Nathan*, ch. 12.
145. *Tanya*, Igeret Hakodesh, sect. 31.

XIII

"What is Hateful to You.."

How does one approach and observe so sensitive and all-comprehensive a *mitzvah* as *Ahavat Yisrael*? There are two principal approaches, both of which are dealt with at length in Chassidut.

The Talmud[146] relates that a would-be proselyte came to Hillel with a request to teach him the whole Torah 'while standing on one leg.' Hillel said to him:

> "*Do not do unto your fellow that which is hateful unto you! This is the whole of the Torah, and the rest is but commentary. Go forth and learn.*"

Rashi offers two interpretations on this statement: (a)

---

146. *Shabbat* 31a.

'Your fellow' refers to G-d. Hillel thus meant to say that just as it is hateful unto you when someone goes against your wishes, so it should be hateful unto you to go against the wishes of G-d. (b) 'Your fellow' is meant quite literally to refer to fellow-beings.

Various commentators[147] already noted that Hillel's dictum raises an obvious question: why would Hillel say what he did in a *negative* form when he could just as well have expressed the same idea in the *positive* form of the Torah's commandment "Love your fellow like yourself"? In fact, however, Hillel's negative wording offers a profound and comprehensive explanation of the Torah's precept:

> "It is said that man does not see his own flaws.[148] This does not mean that he is not aware of his shortcomings. On the contrary, he sees and understands the status of his deficiencies better than anyone else, for another perceives only that which is visible outwardly while he himself discerns what is in the heart. The meaning, then, is that his shortcomings are to him too insignificant to warrant his consideration, and in that sense it is as if he does not see them at all.
>
> "Man's immense sense of self-love causes him to cover up and ignore the very transgressions of which he knows that he is guilty.[149] It encompasses him to the extent that (the awareness of his shortcomings)

---

147. See *Mahrsha, Iyun Ya'akov,* and *Maharatz, ad loc.; Netivot Olam,* Ahavat Re'a, ch. 1 and 3.
148. See *Shabbat* 119a; *Bechorot* 38b. Cf. *Nega'im* 2:5.
149. See Proverbs 10:12.

will not penetrate from the intellectual level of his mind to the emotive level of his feelings. That is why he is not impressed by them at all to the point of doing something about it. In that sense, then, he does not see his own defect, because it has become submerged and nullified in the intense self-love concealing all transgressions..

"Thus when another person sees and becomes aware of his faults, he becomes upset, notwithstanding the fact that he himself knows the truth fully well. His being upset is not on account of thinking that the other imagines a falsehood, for he is himself fully aware of the truth; but rather because his deficiency is real and significant in the perception of the other, while in his own mind it is covered up (i.e., of no consequence whatever) because of his self-love..

"This, then, is the meaning of (Hillel's maxim): *'what is hateful to you'* — that is, this revelation (that others notice your personal faults and regard them as real and significant), *'do not do to your fellow'* — that is, do not regard *his* faults and transgressions as real and significant, whether it be in matters of his social behaviour or his religious conduct. Your love for another is to be so great that it cover his flaws so that the awareness of these will not express itself on a level of emotive reactions.

"This is analogous to an intensely sensed friendship: by virtue of immense affection issuing from the very essence of the soul, one will completely disregard and treat as of no account any wrongdoing of the other which runs counter to this affection, for 'many waters cannot extinguish the love [nor can floods drown it].'[150]

"That is why this principle is 'the whole of the Torah.' For this inclusivity of the souls of Israel, of the one being compounded in the other to become literally unified as if they were but a single entity, effects Above the wondrous result which constitutes the very essence and purpose of the whole Torah: the unity of the Holy One, blessed be He, and His *Shechinah* .. which is the very source of the souls of Israel..

"The absorption of the souls of Israel in one another to become unified brings about the absorption of the one in the One, i.e., that G-d, blessed be He, unifies with Israel to become one. The aspect of *Adam* of Above,[151] therefore, will not see any defect within Himself, as it were, and thus overlook any transgression of Israel, as 'one being cleansed in the mighty sea.'[152] Thus it is written,[153] 'He did not behold iniquity in Jacob and did not see perversity in Israel' — *because* — 'G-d, his G-d, is with him'.. Now the phrases 'He did not behold' and 'did not see' do not mean, Heaven forbid, that (those things) are hidden from Him, for everything is revealed and known to Him, even 'trivial conversations.'[154] It is, rather, as Scripture states, 'He sees iniquity but does not con-

---

150. Song 8:7.
151. See Ezekiel 1:26.
152. *Cf. Zohar* III:132b.
153. Numbers 23:21.
154. *Yerushalmi, Chagigah* 1:2; *Vayikra Rabba* 26:7; *Chagigah* 5a.

sider it;'[155] that is, His infinite and boundless knowledge of these will not manifest itself in the attribute of *gevurah*,[156] because (the attribute of) love covers, and as it is written, '*Elokah* (G-d) screened for him'[157] — (the Divine Name) *Elokah* signifying Supreme love and kindness..[158]

"It is otherwise, though, when, Heaven forbid, there is disunity in Israel. For 'whosoever has a defect shall not approach to offer..' and causes the aspect of division Above.[159] Faults, therefore, will be noted, especially in him — as he is the one who caused the divisiveness, may the Merciful save us from such. But 'Bless us, our Father, all of us *as one*,'[160] for then 'You are altogether (i.e., whole; complete) — (thus) beautiful, My beloved, and there is no blemish in you,'[161] and this effects the unification of the Holy One, blessed be He, and His *Shechinah*..

"That is why Hillel said, 'the rest is but commentary.' For the purpose of all *mitzvot* is to effect the unity of the Holy One, blessed be He, and His

---

155. Job 11:11.
156. *Gevurah* is the Divine attribute of strict justice and judgments; see *Mystical Concepts in Chassidism*, ch. III: sect. 5.
157. Job 3:23.
158. See *Zohar* I:94a and III:23b.
159. See *Sefer Charedim*, I: ch. 7.
160. Liturgy, last blessing of the *Amidah*. The implication is that when we are all together as one, our Father will bless us with the light of His countenance; see *Torah Or*, Esther, p. 97df.; R. Dov Ber of Lubavitch, *Sha'arei Orah*, p. 93af.
161. Song 4:7. See R. Menachem Mendel of Lubavitch (Tzemach Tzedek), *Reshimot al Shir Hashirim*, on this verse.

Shechinah[162] .. which depends on the manifestation of true love to the point of being literally 'like yourself,' for 'His people are part of G-d'..[163] This is achieved through the fulfillment of the *mitzvah* of 'Love your fellow like yourself,' while all the other precepts are like a commentary to explain the various modes of this unity."[164]

---

162. See *Zohar* II:119a; *Reishit Chochmah*, Sha'ar Ha'ahavah, ch. 8f.; *Kissei Melech* on *Tikunei Zohar* 3a, note *shin*.
163. Deuteronomy 32:9.
164. *Derech Mitzvotecha*, s.v. Ahavat Yisrael.

XIV

Soul *vs.* Body

The second approach is offered in *Tanya*. It is based on the premise that all of Israel are interrelated by virtue of their souls, the Divine component in man:

> "Who can know the greatness and excellence of the soul and spirit in their root and source in the living G-d? Moreover, all of them are of one kind and have one Father. Thus by virtue of the (common) source of their soul in the one G-d, all of Israel are literally called brothers.[165] Their bodies alone differ one from the other."

The precept of "Love your fellow like yourself" with respect to every member of Israel, both great and small,

---

165. See above, notes 96-97.

relates to a recognition and appreciation of the soul. The soul is the principal component of man, his very essence, while the body is but secondary. Even as man perceives the body and the soul, so he will perceive others, for there is an intrinsic and most intimate relationship between the souls as they are all rooted in the same source.[166] The bodies, however, differ one from the other.[167] Thus

> "there cannot be true love and brotherhood among those who regard their bodies to be the most significant, while considering their soul to be of secondary importance."

For as they focus on the transitory body, their love, too, is at best transitory, subject to the presence or absence of that which is meaningful to them.[168] On the other hand, those who rejoice but in the joy of the soul alone, and they shrug off the body as a secondary means toward a higher end,[169] will thus find a direct and easy way to attain the fulfillment of the *mitzvah* of *Ahavat Yisrael*.

> "That is why Hillel the Elder said of the observance of this precept that 'this is the whole of the Torah, and the rest is but commentary..' For the foundation and root of the entire Torah is to raise and exalt the soul high beyond the body, up unto the Source and Root of all the worlds, and also to elicit the light of the *En Soph*, blessed be He, unto *Knesset Yisrael*.. i.e., unto the source of the souls of Israel 'to become

---

166. See *Zohar* III:29b, and *ibid.* 123b. Cf. *Tikunei Zohar* 38:79b.
167. Though see above, note 104.
168. See *Avot* 5:16; *Eliyahu Rabba*, ch. 28.
169. See *Tanya*, ch. 31.

one in the One.' This is not possible when there is, Heaven forbid, disunity among the souls. For the Holy One, blessed be He, does not dwell in a place that is blemished.[170] Thus it is said, 'Bless us, our Father, all of us together *as one*, with the light of Your countenance,'[171] as explained at length elsewhere."[172]

Personal humility[173], and an exaltation of the soul over and above the body, clear the path towards a sincere and encompassing *Ahavat Yisrael*. For these prerequisites open the eyes to perceive and sense the Divine element in all, which is essentially the same as the Divine element in oneself. Love of others, love of that which was created and fashioned by G-d, therefore, is tantamount to love of G-d Himself.[174]

---

170. *Zohar* I:216a.
171. See above, note 160.
172. *Tanya*, ch. 32.
173. See *Siddur im Dach*, p. 22c; and see above, notes 111-112.
174. See above, sect. XI; and cf. *Shaloh*, Sha'ar Haoti'ot, s.v. beriyot; *Reishit Chochmah*, Sha'ar Ha'ahavah, ch. 6. See also *Eliyahu Rabba*, ch. 28.

In this context we can readily understand the emphasis Chassidism places upon the precept of *Ahavat Yisrael*. The Baal Shem Tov taught that the essence of a Jew's task is to bring himself to an all-comprehensive love of G-d, love of Torah, and love of Israel (*Butzina Dinehura*; cited in *Sefer Baal Shem Tov*, Mishpatim, par. 17). This is premised on the Zoharic interpretation of the intrinsic unity of G-d, Torah and Israel (*Zohar* III:73a), which is itself based on the identity of the 'concealed aspects' (the 'soul-aspects') of Torah and Israel with Divinity. Thus even as Chassidism is *pnimiyut Hatorah* (the inner dimension of the Torah), the *nishmata deorayta* (the soul of the Torah), it seeks

Conclusion

Prerequisite to Redemption

The recognition and realization of the innate unity and oneness of Israel was the precondition for the revelation at Sinai and the giving of the Torah.[175] It remains also a

---

and emphasizes the soul-aspect in everything. *Ahavat Yisrael*, which is ultimately based on a recognition of Israel's common denominator, i.e. the Divine soul, therefore, is not some tactical or practical approach adopted by Chassidism. It is a an intrinsic part, a logical and indivisible consequence, of the very nature of Chassidism itself and all that it signifies. See also *Sefer Ha'arachim-Chabad*, s.v. Ahavat Yisrael, sect. 9.

175. *Mechilta*, and Rashi, on Exodus 19:2; *Yalkut Shimoni*, Mishlei, par. 934. See *Likutei Sichot*, vol. II, pp. 298 and 301. In this context note also that there are 600,000 root-souls of the people of Israel (see *Tanya*, ch. 37) corresponding to the 600,000 letters of the Torah (see *Zohar Chadash*, Shir:74d). Thus it is also said that the term *Yisrael* is an acrostic for 'Yesh Shishim Ribuy Oti'ot Latorah' (*Megaleh Amukot*, ofan 186; see at length,

requisite for the ascent and acceptance of prayer.[176] And it will bring about the ultimate redemption and Divine manifestation of the Messianic age, as it is written,[177] "You were sold *chinam* (for naught), and you shall be redeemed without money":

> "The Second Temple was destroyed because of the sin of *sinat chinam* (gratuitous hatred).[178] The redemption, therefore, depends on there being peace and our being united as one..[179] For as long as there is *sinat chinam*, the redemption cannot be. Even if there be good deeds in Israel, there cannot be a redemption when there is no peace.
>
> "Our sages interpreted 'The lover of money shall not be satisfied with money'[180] to refer to 'the lover of *mitzvot*.'[181] This, then, is the meaning of 'You were sold *chinam* — for naught' .. for the sin of *sinat chinam*; thus 'without money' — i.e., not by virtue of *mitzvot* 'will you be redeemed.' That is, even if there be many *mitzvot*, but there remains *sinat chinam*, the redemption will not occur."[182]

Nitzutzei Zohar on *Zohar Chadash*, Shir:74d). The implication is clear: every single Jew has his own letter in the Torah, and anything wrong with any one letter in the Torah renders the whole Torah-scroll defective (see *Tikunei Zohar* 25:70a; *Zohar* III:71a; *Likkutei Sichot* (English), vol. III, p. 114*f*.; and *cf. Eruvin* 13a).

176. See above, sect. X.
177. Isaiah 52:3.
178. *Yoma* 9b. See above, sect. XII.
179. See *Tanchuma*, Nitzavim:1.
180. Ecclesiastes 5:9.
181. *Kohelet Rabba* on this verse. *Makot* 10a.
182. Chida, *Chomat Anoch*, on Isaiah 52:3.

Israel cannot be redeemed until they will be united. *Sinat chinam* caused the *galut*. Measure for measure, therefore, *ahavat chinam*, a practice of *Ahavat Yisrael* to the point of *ahavat chinam* — a love of even those that are '*chinam*, i.e., devoid of *mitzvot*,'[183] will bring about the redemption through Mashiach,[184] when the whole world shall be filled with knowledge and awareness of Divinity even as the waters cover the sea.[185]

---

183. See *Sifre* on Numbers 11:5. *Cf.* R. Menachem Mendel of Lubavitch, *Bi'urei Hazohar*, vol. I, p. 248.
184. *Likutei Sichot*, vol. II, pp. 499 and 598.
185. Isaiah 11:9; Maimonides, *Hilchot Melachim* 12:5.

וצדיק יסוד עולם

The Concept Of The *Rebbe-Tzadik* In Chassidism

The Concept of the *Rebbe-Tzadik* in Chassidism

Table of Contents

I	Definition of Terms	85
II	"Of the King's Household"	89
III	"Walking with the Wise"	94
IV	The Stature of *Tzadikim*	99
V	Linking Heaven and Earth	103
VI	Gateway to G-d	107
VII	Heart of Israel	112
VIII	"Reviled, but does not revile.."	116
IX	Individual Responsibility	120

וצדיק יסוד עולם

The Concept Of The *Rebbe-Tzadik* In Chassidism

I

Definition of Terms

The term *tzadik* derives from *tzedek* — righteousness; justice. *Tzadik* thus means a righteous person. The general definition is that of a person who obeys and fulfills G-d's will which is expressed in the precepts of the Torah.[1]

There are, though, various degrees and levels in the category of *tzadikim*.[2] The Talmud thus speaks of a 'good

---

1. *Tanchuma*, Vayera:19; *ibid.*, Vayishlach:2, Vayikra:1, and Emor:5. See also *Megilah* 15b.
2. See *Tanya*, ch. 1; *Likutei Sichot*, vol. IV, p.1235*ff*. Cf. *Sifre*, Ekev, sect. 47.

tzadik,' i.e., one who is good in his relationship to Heaven as well as in his relationship with man; and a '*tzadik* who is not good,' i.e., one who is good in his relationship with Heaven but not with man.[3] There is also '*tzadik vetov lo* (the *tzadik* that has good)' — i.e., the perfect tzadik; and '*tzadik vera lo* (the *tzadik* who has bad)' — i.e., the imperfect *tzadik*.[4] The perfect *tzadik* is defined as one who no longer has any inclination to evil (*yetzer hara*).[5] The imperfect *tzadik* still has a *yetzer hara*, but he is in complete control over it.[6] Then there is a 'figurative' concept of *tzadik*: he whose merits outweigh his faults and defects is legally designated a *tzadik*; that is, for all *legal* purposes of judgment he is found righteous and meritorious.[7]

Another distinction is between the basic definition of *tzadik* as one who does all he is to do, and the one who goes beyond the legal requirements of the law. The latter is usually referred to as *chassid*.[8] The term *chassid* derives from *chessed* — kindness; love. The *chassid* displays not only fear and awe of G-d, total submission to the Divine Will, but "conducts himself with love and benevolence towards his Creator." He follows the Torah purely for the sake of the Divine Will, "like a child that ingratiates itself with its

---

3. *Kidushin* 40a.
4. *Berachot* 7a.
5. As, for example, it is said of King David that he had slain his *yetzer hara*; *Yerushalmi, Berachot* 9:5; *Baba Batra* 17a (cited in *Tanya*, ch. 1). As for Ecclesiastes 7:20, see *Tossafot, Baba Batra* 17a, *s.v.* sheloshah, that this applies to "most people," i.e., the average person; *cf. Zohar* III:276a.
6. *Zohar* II:117b. Cf. ibid. III:273a.
7. *Kidushin* 40b, and Rashi *ad loc.* Maimonides, *Hilchot Teshuvah* 3:1. See *Zohar* III:231a.
8. See *Encyclopaedia Talmudit, s.v.* chassid, for relevant sources.

father and mother, who it loves more than its own body and soul .. and is prepared to sacrifice its own life for them.."⁹

Thus when using the term *tzadik* we must, first of all, distinguish between (a) the figurative sense of the term (which includes one who has sins, but these are outweighed by his virtues and merits), and (b) the essential, literal sense of the term (which applies only to one who is altogether sinless). Secondly, even in the latter category there are (a) imperfect saints (who still possess a *yetzer hara*, albeit totally suppressed to the point of no longer tempting them), and (b) the perfect saint (who no longer has a *yetzer hara* because he has converted and sublimated it into a *yetzer tov*[10]).

The latter distinction follows not only in terms of the definitions given above, but also from a comment by R. Shimon bar Yochai: "I have seen *bnei aliyah* (superior men; superior *tzadikim*), and they are but few."[11] The Talmud questions this by noting the tradition that there are 18,000 *tzadikim* who stand before the Holy One, blessed be He. The discrepancy is resolved by noting that there are differences in the degrees and levels of saintliness. The *perfectly* righteous are but few, but there are many thousands of lower ranks.[11]

The significance of the superior or perfect saints is not only with regards to themselves, but more so with regards to

---

9. *Zohar* III:281a.
10. See *Berachot* 54a; *Sifre*, Va'etchanan, sect. 32.
11. *Sukah* 45b. For other amounts in the number of *tzadikim*, see *Zohar* III:68b (125,000); *Sukah* 45b (1000; 100; 36; 2; 1); *Tikunei Zohar* 21:50b (72); *Chulin* 92b (45); *Yerushalmi, Avodah Zara* 2:3; *Tanchuma*, Vayera:13; *Bereishit Rabba* 49:18 etc. (30).

the world at large. For the world at large exists and subsists by virtue of these *tzadikim*, as it is said, "The *tzadik* is the foundation of the world" (Proverbs 10:25).[12] Thus there is never a generation without such *tzadikim*. They are unique souls like the patriarchs Abraham, Isaac and Jacob, or like Moses.[13] There are, however, not too many of these unique *tzadikim*, while the world needs them in all times. G-d, therefore, "planted them in every generation, as it is said, 'For the pillars of the earth are G-d's, and He has set the world upon them' (I Samuel 2:8)."[14]

This is the concept of *tzadik hador*, the special saint of the generation whose merit protects the world. It does not exclude the existence of other contemporary *tzadikim*, even of perfect ones.[15] Various people, though, may perceive in distinct holy individuals the very personification and role-model of the *tzadik yessod olam* — the *tzadik* who is the foundation of the world, and thus relate to them accordingly.

---

12. *Chagigah* 12b; *Shir Rabba* 7:8. *Midrash Tehilim* 1:15. See also *Sefer Habahir*, par. 157.
13. *Bereishit Rabba* 56:7; ibid., 74:3; *Bamidbar Rabba* 3:1.
14. *Yoma* 38b; see there.
15. See *Likutei Sichot* IV:pp. 1235-8. Cf. *Tzava'at Harivash*, sect. 125 (quoted below, note 102).

II

"Beloved Child in the King's Household"

The true *tzadik* is recognized, even externally, through his special and consistent relationship to G-d and to man. For as he is filled with a consuming love for G-d, he also loves G-d's creation and creatures.[16] His special relationship with G-d may be seen in the following story in the Talmud:

> The son of Rabban Yochanan ben Zakai fell ill, and he asked his disciple R. Chanina ben Dosa to pray for him that he may live. R. Chanina put his head between his knees and prayed for him, and he lived. Said Rabban Yochanan: "If ben Zakai had stuck his head between his knees all day long, no notice would have been taken of him." So his wife asked

---

16. *Cf.* Commentary of Rabad on *Sifra*, Kedoshim 4:12; R. Joseph Albo, *Ikkarim* I:24; *Tossafot Yom Tov*, and *Tanya* ch. 32, on *Avot* 1:12. *Cf.* also *Keter Shem Tov*, Hossafot, par. 141.

him: "Is then Chanina greater than you are?" He replied: "No; but he is like a servant before the king (i.e., like a member of the household with unrestricted access to the king — *Rashi*) while I am like a nobleman before the king (who can enter only at certain times — *Rashi*)."[17]

Thus even the recognized leaders of their generations, like Rabban Gamliel and Rabban Yochanan, would ask R. Chanina to intercede on their behalf.

The same analogy is found with Chuni Hama'agal, who would always be asked to pray for necessary rain. His prayers were effective, too, because he was 'like a beloved child in the King's household.'[18]

The *tzadik* thus stands in an especially close relationship with G-d. By virtue of his standing, he achieves and is endowed with special powers. While G-d retains to Himself the keys for rain, sustenance, revival of the dead, and childbirth, He will grant these to *tzadikim*.[19] In fact, "see how beloved *tzadikim* are unto the Holy One, blessed be He! For whatever they do and decree, the Holy One, blessed be He, confirms and fulfills it."[20] Moreover, the Almighty says, "I rule man. Who 'rules' Me? The *tzadik*! For I make a decree, and he can annul it!"[21]

Thus even while generally a sick person's prayers for

---

17. *Berachot* 34b. See R. Chasdai Crescas, *Or Hashem* III:2-Klal I: end of ch. 2 (cited in *Hakotev* on *Berachot* 34b).
18. *Ta'anit* 19a; *ibid.* 23a.
19. *Tanchuma* (Kadum), Vayetze:16. Cf. *Ta'anit* 2a-b, and *Tossafot ad loc.*
20. *Tanchuma* (Kadum), Va'eira:22; *Bamidbar Rabba* 14:end of 4; *Zohar* I:45b. See also *Shabbat* 59b.
21. *Mo'ed Katan* 16b; *Zohar* I:45b. Cf. *Shabbat* 63a.

The Concept of The Rebbe-Tzadik

himself are more efficacious than those of anyone else,[22] nonetheless it is ruled that whosoever has trouble or a sick person in his house should go to a sage to have him invoke G-d's mercy for him.[23] That is why we find throughout the Talmud and Midrashim (and throughout our tradition) that *tzadikim* have always been approached to pray for the childless, the sick and the troubled, and to seek their counsel and blessing in all matters of concern.[24]

This power of *tzadikim* obviously is not an independent, personal power. It derives from their special attachment to G-d. G-d grants them special consideration because of His reciprocal love for them. The *tzadik*, as stated, has special access, and he knows how to use it to approach G-d properly.

---

22. *Bereishit Rabba* 53:14.
23. *Baba Batra* 116a; *Shulchan Aruch*, Yoreh De'ah 335:10. See *Ta'anit* 8a, to go to 'the *chassid* of the generation.'
24. On the efficacy of the *tzadik's* advice, see below, note 51.

   Note that the thaumaturgic powers of the *tzadik* are not something of the past alone, i.e., restricted to Biblical and Talmudic times, but apply to all times and generations; see the responsum of R. Hai Gaon in *Otzar Hageonim, Chagigah* 14a (p. 13*ff.*), quoted at length in *Hakotev, Chagigah* 14a. See also Tzemach Tzedek, *Sefer Hachakirah*, pp. 99 and 129, and *Sefer Halikkutim*, s.v. yod, p. 1598*f.* See also the Maggid's comment quoted in R. Shelomoh of Lutzk, *Dibrat Shelomoh*, Beshalach, on Exodus 14:27. *Cf.* the Maggid's *Likutei Amarim*, sect. 48, 90, and 134; and *Or Torah*, sect. 54, 91, and 472; on how it is possible for the *tzadik* to overcome the natural order and change things. Note also *Likutei Amarim*, sect. 239, and *Or Torah*, sect. 89 (discussed and explained in *Likutei Sichot*, vol. VI, p. 86*ff.*). *Cf.* R. Elimelech of Liszensk, *No'am Elimelech*, Vayetze (Genesis 30:37), Acharei (Leviticus 18:8), and Emor (Leviticus 23:4). See also below, note 51, about the power of *ru'ach hakodesh* nowadays.

He knows how to submit his requests and prayers.[25] Thus the *tzadik* has the ability to turn the Divine attribute of harshness to that of mercy and compassion[26]: "Woe to the wicked who turn the Attribute of Mercy into the Attribute of Judgment .. Happy are the *tzadikim* who turn the Attribute of Judgment into the Attribute of Mercy."[27]

The *tzadik* will not use his power or privilege for himself. For himself he is content with whatever he has, and he will not use his abilities to improve his own lot: Every day a Heavenly Voice goes forth, proclaiming, "The whole world is sustained by virtue of Chanina [ben Dosa], My son, and Chanina My son suffices himself with a single pot of carobs from the eve of one Shabbat to the eve of the next Shabbat!"[28]

When the *tzadik* intervenes before G-d it is for the sake of the world, for the sake of Israel. When he becomes aware of troubles and trials that are about to come upon the people of Israel, he stands up and protests to G-d![29] To be sure, this may appear as unbecoming arrogance, interfering with Divine judgments and designs. On the human level we would not endure such interference, for "when one says to another, 'Why are you doing this or that,' he would get angry." But when the *tzadik* does so with G-d, He does not get angry and will not punish him for it; for G-d knows that the *tzadik* does not seek any benefit for himself but only for the children of Israel.[30]

---

25. See *Midrash Tehilim* 19:17. *Cf. Vayikra Rabba* 5:8. See also *Zohar* I:41a.
26. *Sukah* 14a.
27. *Bereishit Rabba* 33:3, and *ibid.*, 3:37.
28. *Berachot* 17b. *Ta'anit* 24b, and see there the sequel.
29. *Midrash Tehilim* 77:1.
30. *Midrash Tehilim* 2:2.

The Concept of The Rebbe-Tzadik

The *tzadik* will thus always stand up for Israel. He always judges every person — *any* person — favourably.[31] He will always seek out and point out anyone's merits, and forever find excuses for their failures. For this is precisely what G-d wants to hear, and causes Him to rescind any negative judgments.[32] The *tzadik* sees this as his objective. He is forever conscious of the fact that if one is able to pray on behalf of another and does not do so, he is himself called a sinner.[33]

In this context the *tzadik* is not concerned only with those close to his own ideals, with good and pious people. He will seek out the wicked and sinful to move them to *teshuvah*.[34] He pleads in favour of the wicked in order to still the Heavenly anger.[35] He is conscious of the obligation to pray on behalf of sinners that they repent and return to G-d.[36] His charity, therefore, includes not only help for the materially poor and needy, but also the highest form of *tzedakah*: the spiritual charity of making the wicked meritorious.[37]

---

31. *Avot* 1:6; *Zohar* I:204b. See *Tanchuma*, Shoftim:4; and *cf. Avot deR. Nathan*, ch. 8, and *Shabbat* 127a-b.
32. *Berachot* 32a; *Shemot Rabba* 42:9. Cf. *Tanchuma*, Shoftim:4.
33. *Berachot* 12b.
34. *Zohar* II:128bf. See Maimonides, end of *Igeret Hashemad*; *Sha'arei Kedushah* 2:7; *Sefer Charedim*, Teshuvah, end of ch. 5.
35. *Zohar* I:255a.
36. See *Zohar* I:105a, and *Nitzutzei Orot*, and *Nitzutzei Zohar*, ad loc. See *Sefer Chassidim*, par. 76, and *Mekor Chessed*, ad loc. Cf. *Sanhedrin* 37a.
37. *Zohar* II:129a, and *Nitzutzei Orot*, ad loc. [Cf. "The Dynamics of *Ahavat Yisrael*," notes 54-57, and *ibid*. sect. VII and XI; "The Philosophy of Lubavitch Activism," note 17.]

III

Walking with the Wise

In view of the special and ideal nature of the *tzadik*, it is of great significance to seek his presence, to be associated with him as much as possible. For "'He who walks with the wise, shall be wise' (Proverbs 13:20). This is analogous to entering a perfumery: though one will not sell or buy anything there, nonetheless, when leaving the shop he and his garments will have absorbed the pleasant scent, and this good scent will not depart from him all day long. Likewise, he who associates with *tzadikim* is influenced by their ways and good deeds."[38]

Moreover, while this effect happens of itself, from mere contact and association, the *tzadik* will not suffice

---

38. *Pirke deR. Eliezer*, ch. 25; *Midrash Mishlei*, ch. 13. See *Yalkut Shimoni*, Va'etchanan, par. 824.

with a passive association. He will make every effort to have all others act and do the right things even as he himself does.[39] Little wonder, then, that the Torah makes attachment to *tzadikim* a religious obligation by ordaining to 'cleave unto G-d' (Deuteronomy 11:22): "How is it possible to say that? But cleave unto the sages and it will be accounted to you as though you cleave unto Him."[40]

The term 'sages' referred to, is not simply scholars. For one can be very learned, full of academic knowledge, yet remain unaffected by his studies.[41] To be sure, one is to respect all Torah-scholars.[42] The sages to which one is to attach oneself, however, must be role-models whose scholarship is clearly reflected in their conduct and manners. One should accept as a master only a sage who is like unto an angel of G-d.[43] The codes thus define in detail the character and qualities a true sage must display in both his private and public conduct.[44]

This distinction would seem to follow clearly from the precise wording in Maimonides' Code: "Man must attach himself to *tzadikim* and always dwell with sages, in order to learn from their deeds."[45] Directly relevant to our context,

---

39. *Midrash Hagadol* on Genesis 18:19.
40. *Sifre*, Ekev, sect. 49; Rashi, and *Midrash Lekach Tov*, on Deuteronomy 11:22. Maimonides, *Hilchot De'ot* 6:2. See *Ketuvot* 111b.
41. See *Megilah* 28b; *Zohar* III:275b.
42. *Kidushin* 32b; Maimonides, *Hilchot Talmud Torah* 6:1.
43. *Mo'ed Katan* 17a; *Hilchot Talmud Torah* 4:1. Cf. *Chagigah* 15b.
44. Maimonides, *Hilchot Yessodei Hatorah* 5:11; *Hilchot De'ot*, ch. 5; *Hilchot Talmud Torah* 3:6ff. See *Sifre*, Berachah, sect. 343; and *Shir Rabba* 1:2.
45. *Hilchot De'ot* 6:1.

therefore, is the description of the ideal sage: "..great in wisdom and strong in his character-traits. His *yetzer* never overpowers him in anything at all but he always overpowers his *yetzer* .. He is possessed of a broad and very settled mind .. He enters the *pardes*[46] and continually dwells upon those great and abstruse themes, having the right mind to understand and to grasp. He sanctifies himself and withdraws from the ways of ordinary people who walk in the obscurities of the transient. He zealously trains himself not to have any thoughts of any idle things and transient vanities and their intrigues, his mind constantly turned to Above, bound to beneath the (Heavenly) Throne .. considering the wisdom of the Holy One, blessed be He (as it is displayed throughout His creation).."[47]

Thus it is good to be close to, and associated with, a *tzadik*.[48] For all that is attached to the pure is pure.[49] Happy

---

46. *Pardes* refers to the esoteric teachings of the Torah, as defined in *Hilchot Yessodei Hatorah* 4:13 (*cf.* also "On the Study and Propagation of *Pnimiyut Hatorah*," note 9). The ideal student of Torah will include these in his studies — see *Zohar* III:275b; Maimonides, *Hilchot Talmud Torah* 1:12; *cf.* "On the Study and Propagation of *Pnimiyut Hatorah*," sect. II, and notes 7-10 *ad loc*. Note the statement of the Vilna Gaon that knowledge of *sod* (esoterics) is essential for a proper understanding of *peshat* (exoterics); see his commentary on Mishlei 2:9; and *Even Shelemah* VIII:21.
47. *Hilchot Yessodei Hatorah* 7:1. Cf. *Kuzary* 3:5; and *Moreh Nevuchim* 3:51.
48. *Sukah* 56b.
49. *Baba Kama* 92b. Note that this principle applies to all that is attached to *tzadikim*, to the point that "even as the early *tzadikim* were *chassidim*, so were their beasts *chassidot*!" *Avot deR. Nathan*, end of ch. 8, see there and *Ta'anit* 24a; *Chulin* 7a-b. Cf. *Yevamot* 99b, and *Chulin* 5b. (Cf. below, note 52.)

are the *tzadikim* and those who attach themselves to them.⁵⁰ For as long that Israel is attached to the sages and listens to their words, they merit to acquire both this world as well as the world to come; but when they separate from the sages, they are lost from the world.⁵¹

The benefits incurred through that attachment are not only spiritual, but also material. Any dealings with the *tzadik*, even to come into possession of one of his coins, will of themselves effect blessings.⁵² Indeed, even looking at a

---

50. *Tanchuma (Kadum)*, Bereishit:21; *Tanchuma*, Vayera:9. See *Midrash Lekach Tov*, preamble to Noach.
51. *Pessikta Rabbati*, sect. XI:2; *Yalkut Shimoni* on Song 6:11 (par. 992).

"Listening to their words" refers not only to words of teachings and spiritual exhortation, but also to their counsel and advice even for mundane matters: "All are in need of his [mundane] talk as well as of his teachings. 'Whatsoever he does shall prosper' (Psalms 1:3) — all need his advice, as was the case with R. Eleazar ben Arach who gave counsel and his advise turned out successful. They said to him, 'You are a prophet!' But he answered them, 'I am neither a prophet nor the son of a prophet, but I have a tradition from my masters that any advice given *leshem Shamayim* (for the sake of Heaven) will be fulfilled.' R. Menasya said: This is stated explicitly in Scripture — '[There are many desires in the heart of man,] but the counsel of G-d shall stand' (Proverbs 19:21), i.e., advice wherein is the word of G-d shall stand and be fulfilled;" *Midrash Tehilim* 1:19. See also *Avot* 6:1; and *cf. Zohar* II:6b: "*Ru'ach hakodesh* (the inspiration of the Holy Spirit) sometimes dwells upon prophets and sometimes does not; but *ru'ach hakodesh* never departs from the wise, even for a moment.." Note *Keter Shem Tov*, sect. 312; *Likutei Amarim*, sect. 77, and *Or Torah*, sect. 399, how in these days of the *galut* it is easier to attain *ru'ach hakodesh* than in the time of the *Bet Hamikdash*.

52. See *Bereishit Rabba* 39:11. (*Cf. Baba Batra* 16b.)

This principle relates also to the concept that even the material

tzadik has tremendously positive effects and is of great spiritual significance.[53] Just as the look and gaze of the *tzadik* is of beneficial signifiance, so there is benefit in looking or gazing at a *tzadik*[54]: sick people would be cured by just looking at Abraham;[55] R. Judah Hanassi attributed his superior insight to the fact that he merited to see just the back of R. Meir.[56]

---

properties of the *tzadik* absorb his holiness (*cf.* above, note 49), and reflect this — and its blessings — upon those who come into their possession. The Talmud thus relates that a certain sage merited superior insight by virtue of possessing the walking-stick of R. Meir (*Yerushalmi, Mo'ed Katan* 3:1; see *Likutei Sichot*, vol. IV, p. 1096; and *cf.* below, note 56).

In this context there is also special merit in eating the remainders of the *tzadik*'s food, as it is said of R. Yochanan that he gathered and consumed the crumbs remaining from a *se'udat mitzvah* (meal connected with a *mitzvah*) and said, 'May I be part of those who partook in that meal' (*Yerushalmi, Mo'ed Katan* 2:3; note also *Berachot* 64a, 'He who partakes of a meal at which a sage is present, is as if he feasted on the splendour of the *Shechinah*'). This has been cited as a source for the Chassidic custom of consuming *shirayim* — the left-overs of the food and drink of the *Rebbe-Tzadik* (*cf.* below, note 133), and in particular the wine of *kos shel berachah* (the cup over which he recited the grace after meals) — which is in general a source of blessing (see *Berachot* 51b).

53. R. Eliyahu de Vidas, *Reishit Chochmah*, Sha'ar Hakedushah, ch. 8; *Maharsha* on *Megilah* 28a; *Tzava'at Harivash*, par. 50 (and notes *a.l.*); *Midbar Kedemot, s.v.* tziyur. See also references in next note.
54. *Cf. Esther Rabba* 7:9. In this context note carefully the commentary of Ramban on Numbers 1:45; and Responsa of R. David ibn Zimra (*Radvaz*) III:no. 910 (472). This responsum of Radvaz is so significant to the Chassidic concept of the *tzadik* that R. Aaron of Karlin is said to have urged all pious people to copy and memorize it (see *Si'ach Sarfei Kodesh* I: p. 4)!
55. *Bereishit Rabba* 39:11.
56. *Eruvin* 13b. See also *Yerushalmi, Betza* 5:2.

IV

The Stature of Tzadikim

The stature of *tzadikim* is thus seen to be extraordinarily sublime. They are on the highest level of perfection attainable to created entities, superior even to that of the ministering angels.[57] Like the stars in the heavens who stand over and above the world, sometimes visible and sometimes not, so are the *tzadikim*; and as the stars are pure from the demeaning traits of grudge, hatred, jealousy and strife, so are the *tzadikim*.[58] They sanctify themselves in the Divine Holiness, and in turn a Divine holiness attaches itself to them.[59] They are altogether holy: their body is holy and their

---

57. *Sanhedrin* 93a; *Mishnat R. Eliezer*, ch. 15.
58. *Sifre*, Ekev, sect. 47.
59. *Zohar* III:24b; and *ibid.* 36b.

neshamah is holy of holies,[60] and *ru'ach hakodesh* (holy spirit) rests upon them in this world and in the next.[61]

Tzadikim are a *merkavah* (chariot; vehicle) for G-dliness.[62] That is, just as a chariot has no will of its own but is in total submission to the will and directions of the charioteer, so is the *tzadik* with total self-negation altogether submissive to the Divine Will even with his body and bodily functions.[63] The Torah thus applies theomorphic metaphors to the *tzadik: Tzadikim* are called by the Name of G-d.[64] To see and meet them is tantamount to seeing and meeting the 'Face of the *Shechinah*'. Why are they called the 'Face of the *Shechinah*'? Because the *Shechinah* is concealed within the manifest *tzadik*.[65] Thus one is to go after the *tzadik*, to follow him and to make every effort to secure him for oneself, as it is written, "Let us know, and let us follow, in order to know G-d" (Hosea 6:3), and "My people shall go and say, Come let us ascend to the mount of G-d .. and he will teach us of his ways and we shall walk in his path, for out of Zion shall go forth Torah.." (Isaiah 2:3).[66]

---

60. *Zohar* III:70b.
61. *Zohar* III:55b.
62. Rashi on Genesis 17:22; see R. Mosheh Cordovero, *Pardes Rimonim* 16:6 and 22:3.
63. See *Tanya*, ch. 23 and 34.
64. *Yerushalmi, Bikurim* 3:3; *Zohar* II:38a; *ibid.* 124b, and III:79b. Cf. *Baba Batra* 75b.
65. *Zohar* II:163b. See also *Zohar* I:9a; and *cf. Mechilta* on Exodus 18:12; *Bereishit Rabba* 63:6; *Tanchuma*, Tissa:27. See *Pardes Rimonim* 16:6 and 22:3. Note also *Bereishit Rabba* 86:6, and *Lekach Tov* on Genesis 40:15.
66. *Zohar* II:128b, and *ibid.* III:148a. Note that in Kabbalistic terminology, *Zion* is identified with the aspect of *tzadik*; see *Pardes Rimonim* 23:18; and see *Likutei Amarim*, par. 109 and 120.

These seemingly daring metaphors are explained quite simply in terms of the fact that whatever is attached to something can be referred to by that which it is attached to. A messenger is thus referred to by the name of the one who sent him.[67] This applies to the *tzadikim*. For their mind is always cleaving unto G-d, and just as they are constantly attached to Him, so He is attached to them and never forsakes them.[68]

The *tzadikim* of all times share the common denominator of absolute attachment, commitment and devotion to G-d, Torah and Israel. As such they follow and share in the qualities of the first and greatest leader and shepherd of Israel: Moses. In fact, they are regarded as extensions and reflections of Moses. Thus it is said that there is not a generation without a leader like Moses.[69] This is not simply in terms of an analogy, but in a quite real sense: an extension and emanation of Moses exists in every generation, in every *tzadik*.[70]

This Moses-aspect goes further: Moses had a *neshamah kelalit*, a comprehensive soul. His soul was a root-soul which compounded all the souls of his generation: they were all rooted in his own soul.[71] Thus it is also with the *tzadikim*-leaders of every generation: they, too, are compre-

---

67. R. Bachya, Commentary on Exodus 33:7; see there at length.
68. *Zohar* II:11b. *Cf.* above, note 62, and below, note 76.
69. *Bereishit Rabba* 56:7; *Lekach Tov* on Genesis 22:11; *Zohar* I:25a; and references in next note.
70. *Tikunei Zohar* 69:114a. See also *ibid.* 112a; and *Zohar* III:216b. *Cf.* also *Shabbat* 101b (and parallel passages) as interpreted in *Kissei Melech* on *Tikunei Zohar* 1b.
71. *Shir Rabba* 1:3 (I:64); *Mechilta* on Exodus 15:13. See *Tikunei Zohar* 70:138a; *Zohar* I:25a; and *Zohar* II:191b and III:9a.

hensive root-souls compounding the souls of their respective generations.[72] In this sense they are the leaders and shepherds of their generations in every respect that Moses was in his. For the head of the generation is the whole of that generation.[73]

---

72. See *Zohar* II:47a and 198a; above note 70, and below note 73. Cf. *Tanya*, ch. 2.
73. *Zohar* II:47a. See *Bamidbar Rabba* 19:28; and *Tanchuma*, Chukat:23.

V

Linking Heaven and Earth

In context of the above, all culled from the Talmudic-Midrashic tradition, it is readily seen why mysticism in general, and Chassidism in particular, placed so great an emphasis on the concept of the *tzadik* (or in Chassidic terms, the *Tzadik-Rebbe*). Mysticism in general, and Chassidism in particular, seek to inspire and elevate the people and the world to spiritual heights. They aspire to bring man to an awareness and consciousness of Divine Omnipresence and Providence. The *Tzadik-Rebbe* plays a significant role in this, even beyond that of role-model, teacher and guide.

Kabbalah reads the verse of "*tzadik yessod olam* (the *tzadik* is the foundation of the world)" as identifying the concept of *tzadik* with the *Sefirah* of *yessod*, which serves as the all-inclusive channel through which the Divine attributes manifest themselves below.[74] I-Chronicles 29:11 is interpreted to refer to the Divine attributes of the *Sefirot* from *chessed* to *malchut*. The first five are quite explicit [*gedulah* (i.e., *chessed*), *gevurah*, *tiferet*, *netzach* and *hod*]. The next words, then, namely *ki kol bashamayim uba'aretz* (for all in the heaven and on earth), are taken to refer to the *Sefirah* of *yessod*, and the *Zohar*[75] interprets: for *kol* (all), this refers to *tzadik* (i.e., *yessod*) which is joined with the heaven and the earth. In other words, *tzadik-yessod* is the intermediary joining the heaven (the upper spheres) with the earth. This becomes an extremely important concept in the Chassidic view of the *tzadik*.

The *tzadik* is essentially a spiritual person. His life is altogether spiritual, concentrated in faith in, and reverence and love for G-d.[76] The Baal Shem Tov identified *emunah* (faith) with *devekut* (attachment, cleaving unto G-d).[77] The *tzadik* thus is joined to the spiritual reality. On the other hand, he is also a soul in a body, living in this physical world, which joins him to the earth as well. In that sense, then, the *tzadik* becomes an intermediary, the common denominator, that is able to join the physical and the spiritual, the heaven and the earth. He is the channel by means of which heaven and earth can relate to one another, the means through which Divine emanations are channeled to the world. Thus he becomes and is the foundation of the world. He binds all

---

74. See *Pardes Rimonim* 23:18, s.v. *tzadik*. See also *Mystical Concepts in Chassidism*, ch. IV, sect. 6, s.v. yessod.
75. *Zohar* I:31a. See *Zohar* III:223b.
76. See *Tanya*, Igeret Hakodesh, sect. XXVII. Cf. *Kuzary* 3:5; *Moreh Nevuchim* 3:51.
77. *Keter Shem Tov*, sect. 267 and 310.

… worlds together. All emanations that flow from one world to the other, even from the most high, go through the *tzadik*.

This, the Baal Shem Tov and the Maggid teach, is the meaning of the Heavenly Voice proclaiming "The whole world is sustained *bishvil* (because of) Chanina My son":[78] the whole world is sustained through the *shvil* — the path or channel — of Chanina My son (i.e., the *tzadik*).[79] More specifically:

"There is no generation that does not have a *tzadik* like Moses, compounding within himself the whole generation.. This is the *tzadik* of the generation .. as it is said, 'The *tzadik* is the *yessod* of the world.' The attribute of *yessod* is able to ascend to the upper spheres, and to draw forth and bring down the abundance from above, because it compounds all.[80] So, too, the *tzadik* on earth is like a channel — the effluence from which extends to the whole generation, as our sages said, '*bishvil* of Chanina My son.' That is, R. Chanina extended the abundance, and it was through him that it came to all. Just as everything flows through the *shvil*, so R. Chanina himself was like a *shvil* for the effluence [from Above].

"[The *tzadik*] is like the ladder [in Jacob's dream], of

---

78. See above, note 28.
79. *Keter Shem Tov*, sect. 5 and 256; *Likutei Amarim*, sect. 165; *Or Torah*, sect. 15 (cited below) and 123. [*Shvil* may mean 'because of,' as well as 'in, or through, the path of.' Note also the Maggid's use of the term *tzinor* in *Or Torah*, sect. 44, and the sources cited there in my notes.] This interpretation is found already in *Pardes Rimonim* 32:1 (and see there also 22:3); and in *Shenei Luchot Haberit*, Torah Shebiktav: derush Tzon Yossef.
80. See *Zohar* III:247a.

which it is said, 'Ascended and descended *bo* (on it)' (Genesis 28:12). For just as he is able to bring down the effluence and to extend it, so he is able to cause his whole generation to ascend..

"In this context it is understood that all thoughts of *teshuvah* which arise daily in the minds of the wicked come about through the *tzadik* ... For the angels created by the words of the *tzadik* arouse the whole generation to an awakening of *teshuvah*. This is the meaning of 'The angels of G-d, ascended and descended *bo*' (lit., on it, i.e, the ladder), namely *bo* — through him, that is, literally through the *tzadik*. This way, then, the *tzadik* arouses his generation, because they are all included within him. Thus they are moved to thoughts of *teshuvah*, and the *tzadik* is able to elevate them.."[81]

---

81. *Or Torah*, sect. 15. On the angels created by the *tzadik*'s words, see *Midbar Kedemot* 4:21, *s.v.* dibur.

VI

Gateway to G-d

In the passage just quoted, we have a succinct summary of the Chassidic concept of the *tzadik*. It relates to both the physical and spiritual reality and sustenance of the world and man. For the *tzadik* compounds within himself the root-elements of the world as a whole, as well as of mankind.[82] In that sense, he *is* the world.[83] Opposites, like spirituality and physicality, can only be joined by means of something that has some common aspect with both.[84] This is the *tzadik* who is able to join and bind together all

---

82. See *Likutei Amarim*, sect. 170; *Or Torah*, sect. 231.
83. See *Keter Shem Tov*, sect. 395; *Likutei Amarim*, sect. 100. Cf. *Mechilta* on Exodus 15:13.
84. See R. Ya'akov Yosef, *Tzafnat Pane'ach*, p. 26d, citing the Baal Shem Tov (quoted in *Sefer Baal Shem Tov*, Ekev, par. 72); and cf. *Keter Shem Tov*, sect. 188 and 371.

worlds.[85] As he himself is bound up with G-d on the one hand, and with the worlds on the other, he joins them all to Divinity.[86] Thus he is the intermediary between them, the channel or funnel that serves as the passage-way in both directions:

a) "'His kingship rules *bakol* — over all' (Psalms 103:19). The essential rulership of G-d's blessed Kingship is through the *tzadik*. For he is referred to as *kol*, as it is written 'For *kol* (all) in the heaven and on earth' (I-Chronicles 29:11) — which the *Targum* translates 'joined to the heaven and the earth.' The *tzadik* joins the worlds, this lower world with the upper world, and thereby he draws forth all good effluences from the upper worlds to this world."[87] The *tzadik* in this world, by virtue of having reached the level of *mah*[88] — thus becoming attached to the supernal *chochmah*

---

85. *Or Torah*, sect. 143; *Likutei Amarim*, sect. 166.
86. *Or Torah*, sect. 104.
87. R. Mosheh Elyakim of Koznietz, *Da'at Mosheh*, Bereishit, citing the Maggid. The Maggid refers here to the *Zohar* cited above, note 75, identifying *tzadik, yessod* and *kol*. The word *bakol* (in the prooftext of Psalms 103) is thus read "through *kol*."
88. The term *mah* signifies utter self-negation, as in Exodus 16:7-8. In Kabbalistic terminology it relates to the *Sefirah* of *chochmah* — a word which the *Zohar* (III:235b; also *Tikunei Zohar* 4a and 69:112b) reads as a compound of *ko'ach-mah* — the potentiality of *mah* (see *Mystical Concepts in Chassidism*, ch. IV, s.v. chochmah). The concept of *mah* (especially as signifying *chochmah*) is a central theme in the Maggid's teachings, specifically in the context of the ultimate self-negation which absorbs in the supernal *ayin* (naught). Cf., e.g., *Likutei Amarim* sect. 151 and 162; *Or Torah* sect. 387, and *ibid.*, the sections cited above, note 24.

— becomes the mediary through which the Heavenly abundance comes to this world where he himself exists."[89]

b) Even as the *tzadik* is the *shvil* and *tzinor* for the Divine effluences to the world in general, so he is also an intermediary for the people of his generation to ascend to Divinity.

A common denominator establishes a relationship. On the spiritual level, any commonality, even if limited to a single aspect, already establishes an inherent oneness.[90] When joining different parts of water they become one, because every species attaches itself to its own kind. So, too, the *tzadik* is unified with those who became sanctified through his holiness and is able to raise them along with himself.[91] Moreover, as he is the comprehensive soul of his generation, he can elevate all and everything that is rooted in his soul.[92] By means of his own good deeds and service of G-d he can elevate even the souls of the wicked.[93]

In this context, the *tzadik* will sometimes appear involved with mundane affairs. He is seen engaging in mundane speech or the telling of seemingly inconsequential stories, or otherwise dealing with the masses on their own level. This behaviour would seem incompatible with his sublime status. Externally he appears to have lowered and degraded himself, to have stepped aside from his attachment to G-d. In truth, however, he is and remains in a constant state of

---

89. *Or Torah*, sect. 97; *Likutei Amarim*, sect. 123. See also *Or Torah*, sect. 76; *Likutei Amarim*, sect. 178.
90. *Keter Shem Tov*, sect. 188. See also the sources in note 84.
91. *Or Torah*, sect. 470.
92. *Keter Shem Tov*, sect. 277.
93. *Or Torah*, sect. 487; and see also *ibid.*, sect. 489.

devekut in all he does.[94] His anomalous behaviour is but for establishing a relationship with the simple and the lowly. Thus he is able to raise them to higher levels.[95]

It may happen that some people are so deeply rooted in sin and evil that the *tzadik* is unable to elevate them; nonetheless, he is still able to generate thoughts of *teshuvah* in their minds.[96] In short, the *tzadik* plays a most significant role in the spiritual betterment and the rectification achieved through *teshuvah*.[97]

Indeed, the ideal *tzadik* is the one who extracts the precious from the vile,[98] who causes good to blossom and grow in this world. Our sages thus said, "In the place where the *ba'alei teshuvah* stand, even the wholly righteous cannot stand."[99] This refers also to the ideal *tzadik* just mentioned:

---

94. See above, text relating to notes 76-77; and below, text relating to notes 130-135.
95. This concept of the 'degradation' or 'lowering' of the *tzadik* as explained by the Baal Shem Tov, is an oftcited theme in early Chassidic texts, especially in *Degel Machaneh Ephrayim*. See the quotations in *Sefer Baal Shem Tov*, Bereishit, par. 108, and *ibid.*, notes 86 and 89. See also R. Levi Yitzchak of Berdichev, *Kedushat Levi*, Chaye Sarah, quoting the Maggid.

 This concept is related to the Talmudic dictum that "even the *sichat chulin* (lit. profane, or mundane — thus seemingly casual and inconsequential — talk) of sages is subject to careful study" (*Sukah* 21b) for "even their *sichat chulin* is equivalent to the whole Torah" (*Midrash Mishlei* 1:6). Cf. *Hilchot De'ot* 2:4 and 5:1.
96. See references cited above, note 93.
97. Note carefully *Keter Shem Tov*, sect. 270 and 397. See *Degel Machaneh Ephrayim*, Shemini, and *ibid.* Metzora (cited in *Sefer Baal Shem Tov*, Ekev, notes 50 and 52).
98. See Jeremiah 15:19.
99. *Berachot* 34b.

he is called *ba'al teshuvah*, in the literal sense of being the holder and master of *teshuvah*.[100] For he brings people back to goodness, turning many away from sin,[101] generating *teshuvah* in the world. Thus he transcends by far the other type of *tzadik* whose concern is but with his own self-perfection, though the latter, too, is wholly righteous.[102]

How apt, then, the Baal Shem Tov's interpretation of Psalms 118:20: "'This is the gate to G-d — *tzadikim*,' i.e., *tzadikim* are the gate to G-d!"[103]

---

100. *Cf. Zohar* II:106b.
101. Malachi 2:6. *Cf. Avot deR. Nathan*, ch. 12.
102. *Tzava'at Harivash*, sect. 125; *Or Torah*, sect. 257. *Cf. Zohar* I:67b, 106a, and 254b.
103. *Butzina Dinehura*, p. 25a (cited in *Sefer Baal Shem Tov*, Ekev, note 50). *Cf. Zohar* I:150b, and *Or Hachamah ad loc. Cf.* also *Bereishit Rabba* 69:7, and *Midrash Sechel Tov*, on Genesis 28:17.

VII

Heart of Israel

To be sure, and this cannot be over-emphasized, Judaism rejects altogether the idea of any independent power or agency outside of G-d or associated with G-d. There is no intermediary intervening between man and G-d. Man can and must relate to G-d directly. There is no hierarchy in which angels, planets or stars, the so-called 'natural forces', or whatever, might be seen as interposing between man and G-d.[104] The *tzadik* thus never assumes the status of a separate or independent force. His status derives exclusively from his total and absolute submission and attachment to G-d. As

---

104. See *Yerushalmi, Berachot* 9:1; Maimonides, Principles of the Faith, principle 5; *idem, Hilchot Avodah Zara* ch. 1 and 2:1; *Ikkarim* II:28, and *ibid.* IV:16-17; Abarbanel, *Rosh Amanah*, ch. 12; R. Menachem Mendel of Lubavitch, *Derech Mitzvotecha*, Milah, ch. 3. *Cf.* also *Yoma* 52a, and Rashi *ad loc.*

already stated, he has attained the level of being totally free of *yetzer hara*, thus also of any sense of ego. When we speak of the *tzadik* as an intermediary, it is exclusively in the sense of helping man to become bound up in the Divine.

Thus it is said of Moses, "When they have a matter, they come to me" (Exodus 18:16), "You be for the people to G-d-ward (Rashi: messenger and interceder between them and G-d)" (Exodus 18:19) [and "I stood between G-d and you at that time to tell you the word of G-d" (Deuteronomy 5:5)]. In that very same sense the *tzadik* is the intermediary between G-d and the people, and the people and G-d, to join and elevate the people.[105] Our sages thus taught:

"'They believed in G-d and in Moses' (Exodus 14:31). If they believed in Moses, surely they must have believed in G-d? But this teaches you that whoever believes in the shepherd of Israel is the same as having faith in Him who spoke and the world came into being. In like manner you must say, 'The people spoke against G-d and against Moses' (Numbers 21:5): if you say they spoke against G-d, surely they spoke against Moses? But this comes to teach you that speaking against the shepherd of Israel is like speaking against Him who spoke and the world came into being."[106]

The *tzadik* — the shepherd of his generation, the Moses of his generation — like Moses brings the people to belief [and as cited above,[107] belief and faith means *devekut*] in G-d. He elevates them and attaches them to G-d. He is

---

105. See R. Yaakov Yossef, *Ben Porat Yossef*, Introduction, p. 9b*ff*.; *Tzafnat Pane'ach*, p. 113b*f*.
106. *Mechilta* on Exodus 14:31.
107. Text relating to note 77.

merely like a ladder through which it is easy to ascend. In that sense, then, he may be referred to as an intermediary, and nothing beyond that!

In this same context the Torah commands that we must attach ourselves to the sages. And in this same context, too, the Torah enjoins the precept "You shall fear *et Hashem* (G-d)" (Deuteronomy 6:13). The seemingly superfluous word *et* is inserted to include the sages.[108] For as the sages are the very personification of attachment and fear of G-d, association with the sages instills a reflection of their own attachment and reverence. As the reverence of the sage derives exclusively from what he represents as a 'man of G-d,' it must lead to reverence of G-d and makes that ultimate goal so much easier.[109]

The concept of the *tzadik* as the intermediary *shvil* or *tzinor* actually has a striking and quite explicit precedent in the teachings of the Talmud and Midrashim:

The Land of Israel in general, and Jerusalem in particular, are the very heart and center of the world as a whole.[110]

---

108. *Pesachim* 22b; see commentaries *ad loc.*
109. *Keter Shem Tov*, sect. 153 and 181.

In this context we can readily understand the *halachah* and practice to ask *tzadikim* to pray in our behalf (see above, text relating to notes 17-24) without violating the objection to intermediaries; see R. Mosheh of Tirani (*Mabit*), *Bet Elokim*, Sha'ar Hatefilah, ch. 12; and R. Judah Loew (*Maharal*), *Netivot Olam*, Netiv Ho'avodah, ch. 12. See there also about the tradition to pray at the gravesites of *tzadikim* that they should intercede in our behalf (see *Ta'anit* 16a and 23b; *Sotah* 34b; *Zohar* III:70b*ff.*, and the sources cited *ad loc.* in *Nitzutzei Zohar*).

110. *Tanchuma*, Kedoshim:10; *Zohar* III:161a, and *ibid.* 221b. See

The life-force for the world, all blessings and emanations from Above, therefore, issue to all countries through Jerusalem and the Land of Israel.[111] They are the *shvil* for the earth at large, even as they are also the very Gate through which all ascend to Heaven.[112]

It is the same with the people of Israel. It is the very heart of all mankind.[113] Thus Israel is the channel for the sustenance and all blessings of the world.[114] The world exists and subsists only *bishvil Yisrael* — by virtue of, and through the channel of Israel.[115]

In analogous terms, the *tzadik*, the leader and shepherd of Israel, is the very heart of all the people of Israel.[116] Thus he is the very specific *shvil* and *tzinor* connecting Above and below.

---

also *Zohar* I:84b and II:157a. *Cf.* R. Judah Halevi, *Kuzary* II:8-12.
111. *Sifre*, Ekev, sect. 40 and 42; *Ta'anit* 10a.
112. Genesis 28:17, and see *Midrash Hagadol ad loc.* See also *Pirkei deR. Eliezer*, ch. 35.
113. *Zohar* III:221b; *ibid.*, 234a. See *Kuzary* II:8-12 and 36.
114. *Sifre*, Ekev, sect. 40 and 42; *Yerushalmi, Shevi'it* 4:3 and 5:4; *Zohar* II:151b.
115. *Ta'anit* 3b; *Avodah Zara* 10b; *Zohar* II:5b.
116. *Tikunei Zohar* 21:50b. *Cf.* Maimonides, *Hilchot Melachim* 3:6, and *cf.* also *ibid.* 2:6.

VIII

"Reviled, but does not revile.."

When considering this significance and centrality of the *tzadik*, however, there appears to be a problem. From the days of the very first leader and shepherd of Israel, Moses, there has generally always been some opposition to the *tzadik*-leader. He was not always properly recognized by all in his generation. Oftentimes he arouses enmity, jealousy and opposition. This happens not only in terms of plain people, who may not understand and realize what he signifies. Quite frequently the oppostion comes also, and especially so, from scholars and leaders[117] who, we would assume, should know better. This raises an obvious question: if the *tzadik* is so central, the very channel between Heaven and earth through which flow all emanations affecting everyone, why should there be such opposition to him?

---

117. *Cf.* Numbers 16:1-2, and *Tanchuma ad loc.*

THE CONCEPT OF THE REBBE-TZADIK

The Chassidic masters explain that this is part of the Providential design and plan. Thus teaches the Baal Shem Tov:

> Sometimes we see that the *tzadik* is reviled, in a quite contemptuous way. This, however, may be a token of kindness from G-d. For the '*samach-mem*'[118] is extremely envious of the *tzadik* and wishes to lead him astray. G-d, therefore, causes people to malign the *tzadik*. For as the '*samach-mem*' sees how people do so, his jealousy is deflected. Thus it is said, "[..those who speak maliciously against the *tzadik*, with arrogance and contempt.] How abundant is Your goodness which You have hidden away for those that revere You — " (Psalms 31:19-20); that is, "You have hidden and concealed" Your *tzadikim* so that the world at large does not recognize that they are great *tzadikim*, and therefore maligns them. This is the "abundance of Your goodness," because it deflects the jealousy of the '*samach-mem*'.[119]

In a similar vein the Baal Shem Tov interprets the verse, "For what worthlessness have You created all the sons of man" (Psalms 89:48) as a complaint of the *yetzer hara* and

---

118. *Samach-mem* is an abbreviation for the guardian-angel of Esau and Edom (*Zohar* I:170a; *ibid.* III:246b; and *Zohar Chadash*, Noach, 23d; Rashi on *Sukah* 29a), identified with *yetzer hara* (*Zohar* II:42a) and Satan, the chief-denouncer and indictor of Israel (*Shemot Rabba* 18:5; *Devarim Rabba* 11:9).

119. R. Reuven Halevi Horowitz, *Duda'im Basadeh*, Noach (cited in *Sefer Baal Shem Tov*, Korach, note 4). The conventional translation of our prooftext "How abundant is Your goodness, which You have hidden away for those that revere You .. in the sight of men" is thus changed to read: "How abundant is Your goodness, that You have hidden away those that revere You .. in the sight of men."

G-d's reply: When a holy soul is to descend from Above to become vested in a human body, the *'samach-mem'* is incited: he argues that this would incapacitate him from his function to try and seduce people and to lead them astray. For as the *tzadik* will turn the world to goodness, the *yetzer hara* complains, "for what worthlessness have You created [me]?" The Heavenly reply is, "all the sons of man": corresponding to the wise who reprove and discipline there are the 'wise to do evil.'[120] That is, to balance the presence of the *tzadik* (whose very presence and deeds are convincing proof for the truth of G-d and Torah), there will be created an evil man in the form of a scholar and *tzadik* — who will mock the true *tzadik* and negate his words. As this evil person has the outer appearance of a scholar and righteous person, people have an option to attach themselves to him or to the true *tzadik*. This preserves the principle of freedom of choice.[121]

The true *tzadik*, however, will not respond to his opponents. His consciousness is of his cosmic mission and purpose, and not of personal considerations or petty arguments. He is of those "who are insulted but do not insult, hear themselves reviled but do not answer, act through love and rejoice in suffering."[122] For this is of the essential

---

120. See Jeremiah 4:22.
121. *Keter Shem Tov*, sect. 148, in brief. For the lengthy original see *Toldot Ya'akov Yosef*, Shoftim, and also ibid., Behar (see *Sefer Baal Shem Tov*, Korach, p. 145*ff*., and *ibid*. p. 142, note 4).

    For more on opposition to *tzadikim* see R. Elimelech of Liszensk, *Likutei Shoshanah* on *Avot* 5:17; and *Igeret Hakodesh* by his son, appended to *No'am Elimelech*.
122. *Shabbat* 88b. See also *Baba Kama* 93a.

character-traits of the true Torah-sage, of the *tzadik*.[123]

Moses, the role-model for the *tzadikim*-leaders of all generations, disregarded all personal insults. He excelled in being "most humble of all men on the face of the earth" (Numbers 12:3), regarding himself more lowly than even the lowest of man.[124] Humility is the very test and touchstone for the *tzadik*, for, in the words of the Baal Shem Tov, humility increases proportionally to growth in holiness.[125] The Baal Shem Tov established "an important principle: When people insult you .. do not answer them, even in a positive way, in order to avoid being drawn into quarrels, or into pride which causes one to forget the Creator. Our sages thus said that man's silence leads to humility."[126] Silence in the face of insult and curses is the very sign and definition of the true *chassid*.[127]

---

123. *Hilchot Yessodei Hatorah* 5:11; *Hilchot De'ot* 5:13. Cf. note 44.
124. *Likutim Yekarim* (teachings of the Baal Shem Tov, the Maggid, and others), sect. 1.
125. R. Eleazar Halevi Horowitz, *No'am Magadim*, Massey (cited in *Sefer Baal Shem Tov*, Beshalach, note 13; see also *ibid.*, par. 15).
126. *Tzava'at Harivash*, sect. 49; see the notes there.
127. *Midrash Tehilim* 16:11; and *ibid.*, 86:1.

 This, indeed, is the approach of the Baal Shem Tov and his disciples towards those that persecuted them; see, e.g., the Baal Shem Tov's letter to R. Ya'akov Yosef in *Hatamim*, p. 444 (V:p. 20, no. 110); and letters of R. Shneur Zalman of Liadi in *Igrot Kodesh-Admur Hazaken*, nos. 32, 37 (=*Tanya*, Igeret Hakodesh, no. 2), and 41. In this same context it is noteworthy to refer to Rambam's identical reaction to his opponents as evident from his moving letters to Ibn Gabir and Ibn Aknin — *Kovetz Teshuvot Harambam Ve'igarotov*, ed. Leipzig, II:pp. 16d, 30c and 31aff., and see there also part I: no. 140.

 Though the *tzadik* has it in his power to bring punishment upon

IX

Individual Responsibility

In summary, attachment to the *tzadik* is a most significant principle. It helps man ascend on the ladder of piety and holiness to his preordained goal of attachment to G-d. It offers man concrete means to remain forever aware of ultimate reality, of his ultimate nature and purpose in life. The *tzadik* is a physician of the soul, providing both preventative and therapeutic medicine for man's soul.[128] He is *talpiyot* — the elevation for all to turn to.[129] Thus just to meet and see

---

his opponents, he will seek to avoid that by all means in line with the Scriptural principle that "it is not good for the *tzadik* to punish" (Proverbs 17:26); see *Berachot* 7a; *Shabbat* 149b; *Rosh Hashanah* 16b; and *Sefer Chassidim*, sect. 76. Cf. *Keter Shem Tov*, sect. 75; and *Sefer Baal Shem Tov*, Noach, par. 156-7, and the notes ad loc.

128. Cf. *Hilchot De'ot* 2:1; *Shemonah Perakim*, ch. 3.

129. *Tikunei Zohar*. Add., 6:145b (cf. *Berachot* 30a), referring to

the *tzadik* is itself already a profound lesson in Torah-study and Torah-conduct.

R. Leib Sarah's, therefore, would travel far to see the Maggid just to observe how he ties and unties his shoelaces.[130] For the true *tzadik* is an altogether holy personality, the personification of "Let all your deeds be for the sake of Heaven."[131] He personifies the ideal of "Know Him in all your ways" (Proverbs 3:6): "*da'eihu* (know Him) is a word signifying attachment,"[132] attachment to G-d and for the sake of G-d, "in all your actions — even the physical and material ones," such as eating, sleeping, engaging in business, and so forth.[133]

This ideal, however, applies not only to the *tzadik* but to every individual. The same R. Leib Sarah's was wont to say that man's purpose is not just to *study* Torah, but to *become* a Torah. All one's doings, every thought, motion, speech and act, must reflect and personify Torah.[134] R. Shneur Zalman of Liadi, too, said of his master, the Maggid of Mezhirech: elsewhere one learns to master the Torah, i.e., how one is to study Torah; in Mezhirech, however, one

---

Song 4:4 "built as *talpiyot*"; and see *Targum*, and *Tzror Hamor*, on this verse. See also the other commentaries there, interpreting *talpiyot* as a landmark for all to gaze at and use as reference-point for travelers to determine their direction, a source for teaching, instruction and inspiration.
130. *Seder Hadorot Hechadash*, p. 45 (21a).
131. *Avot* 2:17.
132. See *Tikunei Zohar* 69:99a; *Likutei Amarim*, sect. 236; *Or Torah*, sect. 369; *Tanya*, ch. 3.
133. *Tzava'at Harivash*, sect. 94; *Keter Shem Tov*, sect. 282; *Or Torah*, sect. 252. See *Hilchot De'ot* 3:3. Cf. *Tzava'at Harivash*, sect. 98-99; *Likutei Amarim*, sect. 236; *Or Torah*, sect. 369.
134. *Seder Hadorot Hechadash*, p. 45 (21a).

learns to let the Torah master you, i.e., how the Torah teaches man to become a Torah himself.[135]

The *Rebbe-tzadik* helps man achieve this goal. He is essentially a guide, mentor, and teacher. He is a soul-doctor and a role-model who helps and inspires his followers and ignites their souls with the fire of reverence and love for G-d. He unites their souls with the soul of the Torah, and thus with G-d.

As each individual is obligated to reach spiritual perfection, Chassidism cautions that one is not to make oneself completely dependent on the *tzadik*. One is not to rely on him altogether. Everyone must also take the initiative on his own and assume responsibility for the goal of achieving self-elevation. Each one must learn to stand on his own two feet, work on himself, and not rely on the merits and blessings accruing through the *tzadik*. Thus taught the Baal Shem Tov:

In a certain land there was a mighty warrior, and all the people of the land put their trust in him. They did not themselves learn how to wage war because they relied on this mighty warrior. But once there was a war, and the enemy cunningly stole the weapons of that warrior, one by one, until he had nothing left to fight with. Thus even as he was seized, so were all the others who had relied on him.. This is the meaning of, "Happy are the people who *know* the blowing of the *teru'ah* — " (Psalms 89:16): when the people will not rely on the warrior, but will themselves know the *teru'ah* of war, then "they shall walk in the light of Your

---

135. R. Yosef Yitzchak of Lubavitch, *Likutei Diburim*, vol. II, p. 492.

countenance, G-d" (Psalms *ibid.*). For they do not rely on the great ones alone.[136]

The Midrash[137] has a parable about the king of the beasts being angry with his subjects, and the latter looked for someone to appease the king. The fox offered that he would go with them to appease the king with his knowledge of three hundred fables. So they went with him, but in the middle of the way he told them that he forgot half of those fables. They said to him: "The remaining fables will suffice." As they went further, he said that he forgot some more. Again they answered that the ones he retained will suffice. Thus they came to the courtyard of the king, when the fox said that he forgot everything, and that everyone will just have to appease the king as best as he can..

The intent of the wise fox was all along that the others should go and submit to the king and appease him by themselves; but if he had not dealt with them the way he did,

---

136. *Keter Shem Tov*, sect. 33 and 261. [For this emphasis on the word "know" (as opposed to "blow" or "hear"), see *Zohar* III:18b, and *ibid*. 149b and 231b.] In this context, the *tzadik* will oftentimes withdraw and conceal himself and his powers in order to cause the people to take the initiative on their own. While still effecting benevolence, he will do so in a concealed and transcendent way that will not be seen or noticed, for precisely that reason. Thus he will instill the principle of 'eating the toil of your own hands' (Psalms 128:2), i.e., that "G-d will bless you in all *you* do" (Deuteronomy 15:18), which *Sifre* on this verse (Re'ey, par. 123) interprets: "I might think that the thing will come even when man is idle; Scripture thus says, 'In all you do'!" Cf. *Mechilta* on Exodus 20:9; *Avot deR. Nathan* 11:1; and *Zohar* I:88a. See *Likkutei Sichot* (English), vol. II: Shemot, Vayakhel-A.
137. *Bereishit Rabba* 78:7.

they would not have gone with him .. When he said that he had forgotten everything, their hearts broke because they no longer had someone to rely on, and thus each one was compelled to make an effort to appease the king on his own.. Thus I heard from my master [the Baal Shem Tov] a parable for the principle that people should not rely on those who lead the prayers on the *yamim nora'im* (High Holidays), but everyone must make an effort to pray for himself: Once there were two kings battling one another. One of them was mighty and powerful and had mighty soldiers dressed in body-armour.. The other king searched for mighty soldiers like his opponent's but did not succeed .. until in the end he had to tell his army not to rely on mighty warriors..[138]

The *tzadik*'s disciples and followers must realize this responsibility.[139] It is not only a theoretical ideal but a practical and viable goal: when setting their mind and will on this goal, they shall succeed in achieving it. For the Baal Shem Tov and the Maggid teach a basic principle: wherever man's thought and will are, that is where he is himself.[140]

---

138. The first part of this passage (the paraphrase of the Midrash) is quoted in *Keter Shem Tov*, sect. 35; and the latter part (the parable of the Baal Shem Tov) in *Sefer Baal Shem Tov*, Rosh Hashanah, p. 260, par. 3. For the whole passage see *Ben Porat Yosef*, p. 44b.
139. See also *Or Torah*, sect. 455, for a critique of those who lack personal achievement and depend completely on the *tzadik*.
140. *Keter Shem Tov*, sect. 56, 208, 275, and *ibid.*, Hossafot, par. 38, note 42; *Tzavaat Harivash*, par. 69 (and the notes there). *Likutei Amarim*, sect. 93; *Or Torah*, sect. 69. — On this principle of individual responsibility, see also "The Philosophy of Lubavitch Activism," sect. VII.

"Serve G-d With Joy":

On Overcoming Anxiety and Gloom

"Serve G-d with Joy..":
On Overcoming Anxiety and Gloom

Table of Contents

Letter of the *Tzemach Tzedek* 000

Appendix 000

Introduction: The Principle of *Simchah* 129

Letter of the *Tzemach Tzedek* 142

Appendix 148

"Serve G-d With Joy":
On Overcoming Anxiety and Gloom

I

A classic Chassidic maxim, attributed to R. Aaron of Karlin, states that *atzvut* (dejection; depression; melancholy; sadness) is not itself a sin, yet may lead to consequences which the worst sin could not cause.

Atzvut is rooted in self-centeredness: it derives from a sense of, and obsession with, the ego and consequent pursuit of self-gratification. The disappointment and discontent from seeing personal ambitions unfulfilled or frustrated, results in feelings of depression.[1] Indeed, *atzvut* is said to be an aspect of *avodah zara* (idolatry), as evident from the fact that a person in a state of *atzvut* will harbour idolatrous

---

1. See *Tanya*, ch. 27. *Cf.* R. Menachem Mendel of Lubavitch, *Or Hatorah — NaCh*, vol. I, on I-Chronicles 16:27, p. 709, that *simchah* (joy) and *anavah* (humility) are one entity, the latter deriving from the former, while *gassut haru'ach* (arrogance) is the very source and sustenance for *atzvut*; see there at length.

thoughts.[2] Invariably it sets the stage of rationalizing anomalous and improper behaviour to the point of surrendering to base passions and crude self-indulgence.[3]

Little wonder, then, that our sages are highly critical of the trait of *atzvut*.[4] They condemned it as repugnant, and as a major cause of all evil dispositions,[5] aside of the fact that it prevents man from fulfilling his obligation to serve G-d with joy.[6]

---

2. R. Kelonimos Kalman of Cracow, *Ma'or Vashamesh*, on Numbers 11:1. Note R. Menachem Mendel of Vitebsk, *Pri Ha'aretz*, Matot-Massey, that the word *atzav* is a term for both idolatry (as in Psalms 115:4) and *atzvut*.
3. *Ma'or Vashamesh*, ibid.; *Tanya*, beg. of ch. 1, and ch. 26.
4. *Tanya*, Igeret Hakodesh, sect. XI.
5. See R. Chaim Vital, *Sha'arei Kedushah* 1:2, enumerating *atzvut* as one of the four principal dispositions of evil. Also *ibid.* 2:4: "*Atzvut* causes a desistance from the service of observing the *mitzvot*, negates occupation with Torah and concentration in prayer, and nullifies the good intent to serve G-d. It is the gateway to enticing the entrapments of the *yetzer hara* — even for a person that is a *tzadik*..;" see there at length, and also below, note 18.
6. *Sha'arei Kedushah* 2:4; *Tanya*, beg. of ch. 1.

   Note Rambam, *Hilchot Lulav* 8:15: "The joy with which man is to rejoice in the fulfillment of precepts and in the love of G-d who commanded them is a supreme act of Divine worship. Whoever refrains from this rejoicing deserves to be punished, as it is said, 'Because you did not serve G-d, your G-d, with joy and gladness of heart.' (Deuteronomy 28:47) Whoever is arrogant, imparts honour to himself and is concerned with his dignity on such occasions, is a sinner and a fool. Solomon warned about this when he said, 'Do not glorify yourself in the presence of the King.' (Proverbs 25:6) On the other hand, whoever humbles himself and makes light of himself on such occasions, is the honoured great one who serves (G-d) out of a sense of love. David, king of Israel, thus said, 'I will be demeaned yet more than this, and I will be base in my own eyes.' (2 Samuels 6:22)

Numerous texts caution to beware of anything that may lead to gloom, dejection or anxiety. We must generate *simchah* (joy; happiness; cheerfulness), both as an end in itself as well as a means toward the end of observing Torah and *mitzvot* with joy and gladness of heart. For the presence of *simchah* is no less than the very touchstone for the sincerity and authenticity of our involvement with Torah and *mitzvot*.[7]

Greatness and honour are achieved only by rejoicing before G-d, as it is said, 'King David was hopping and dancing before G-d.' (2 Samuel 6:16)" *Cf. Zohar* I:216b and III:56a; and see R. Chaim Chizkiyahu Medini, *Sedei Chemed: Kelalim, s.v.* aleph:326, and shin:25 and 28.

7. R. Eliyahu de Vidas, *Reishit Chochmah*, Sha'ar Ho'ahavah, ch. 10 (p. 103a): "A *mitzvah* performed from the goodness of the heart does itself give joy." For it is a Scriptural decree that "The precepts of G-d are just, *causing the heart to rejoice*" (Psalms 19:9); see *ibid.*; also the Baal Shem Tov's reference to this verse in *Darkei Tzedek*, p. 18a (quoted in notes on *Tzava'at Harivash*, sect. 29); and R. Eliyahu of Smyrna, *Shevet Mussar*, ch. 10. For "*Simchah* is of the side of *kedushah* (holiness);" *Derech Emet* on *Zohar* II:281a. "There is *simchah* and there is *atzvut*: the one is life, the other death; the one is goodness, the other evil; the one is *Gan Eden*, the other *gehenom*. In all things the one is the opposite of the other;" *Zohar* II:255a.

The Torah thus states explicitly that the troubles of the *tochachah* came about "Because you did not serve *Hashem*, your G-d, with joy and gladness of heart — *merov kol*" (Deuteronomy 28:47). That is, the punishment is said to depend on not serving G-d with *simchah*, and not on not serving Him at all! (R. Joseph Albo, *Ikkarim* III:33). Moreover: the conventional translation of *merov kol* is "for the multitude of all," i.e., *whilst* you had all good things. R. Yitzchak Luria, however, interprets: "Because you did not serve G-d with a joy and gladness of heart *exceeding* the joyfulness and gladness of heart in having all good things"! See R. Chaim Vital, *Sha'ar Ru'ach Hakodesh*, p. 33; R. Eliyahu de Vidas, *Reishit Chochmah*, Sha'ar Ho'ahavah, ch. 10 (p. 101b); *Tanya*, ch. 26. *Cf.* above, note 6.

Acts in which the soul rejoices before doing them as well as thereafter, are good; those which cause it pain and sorrow after they are done, are bad.[8] There is thus the simple test of the joy filling man after a good deed indicating that it was proper behaviour.[9] *Simchah* gives completeness to a *mitzvah* in order that the purpose intended by it may be attained; for *simchah* gives completeness and perfection to that which is done.[10]

The principle to beware of *atzvut* and to pursue joyfulness, to have the heart rejoice in G-d, is fundamental in Chassidic thought and tradition.[11] The Baal Shem Tov taught that Chassidim must view *atzvut* as an outright transgression of Torah, and *simchah* [in the sense of finding in everything that quality of goodness which causes joy] as a *mitzvah* of the Torah.[12]

---

8. *Ikkarim* III:6, see there at length. Note R. Judah Loew (Maharal), *Chidushei Agadot* on *Gitin* 70a, 'Anxiety weakens the strength of man': "Anxiety weakens the strength of the soul because the soul's strength derives from being in a state of joy and happiness; for it is known that *simchah* is the very energy of the soul!"
9. R. Ya'akov Yosef of Polnoy, *Tzafnat Pane'ach*, p. 37d (citing *Ikkarim*).
10. *Ikkarim* III:33, see there at length.
11. See *Tzava'at Harivash*, sect. 15: "The third thread .. to distance oneself from *atzvut* as much as possible!" *Ibid.*, sect. 46: "*Atzvut* is a repugnant trait and an obstacle to the service of the Creator .. One must strengthen oneself to rejoice in the Creator .. All these are basic principles, more desirable than much fine gold; every detail is a basic principle!" *Keter Shem Tov*, sect. 302: "The principal thing is to remove *atzvut* and to hold on to *simchah*." Also, "The main thing is to go always with *simchah* .. for without *simchah* it is impossible to be attached to the blessed Creator;" *Likutim Yekarim*, sect. 53 (*cf. Reishit Chochmah, ibid.*, p. 103b).
12. *Keter Shem Tov*, Hossafot, par. 169.

II

This is not to say that *simchah* is a self-sufficient and exclusive disposition in the service of G-d. *Simchah* must be joined by an initial *yirah*, fear and awe of G-d.[13] For *simchah* without *yirah* turns into frivolity marked by unrestrained levity,[14] just as *yirah* without *simchah* is *marah shechorah*, melancholy and gloom.[15]

By the same token, this is also not to say that sadness *per se* is necessarily wrong and evil. Sincere regret and repentance for sins committed — must arouse feelings of discomposure and sorrow, distressing and perturbing the mind over one's failures and shortcomings.[16] A fine distinction is thus drawn between *atzvut* and *merirut* (sense of

---

13. *Or Torah*, sect. 59. See *Midrash Tehilim* 100:3 (and editor's note 13 *ad loc.*); and below, note 22.
14. *Ibid.*; and see there also sect. 124 and 235. Cf. *Tzava'at Harivash*, sect. 128.
15. *Tzava'at Harivash*, sect. 110. See *Likutim Yekarim*, sect. 42.
16. See Rambam, *Hilchot Teshuvah* 1:1 and 2:2-4; *Tanya*, Igeret Hateshuvah, ch. 7.

bitterness). *Atzvut* implies a state of dullness, of being listless and inert, the heart being dull like a rock and devoid of life, of vitality. *Merirut* implies a broken heart, but there remains vitality which ferments agitation: one is embittered about the present condition and agitated by it to the point of doing something about it, to correct and rectify it.[17]

The inertia of *atzvut* is tied in with a 'heaviness of the spirit.' It is tantamount to laziness and sluggishness, in which one surrenders to the mood, resigns himself to his present state. In that frame of mind there is despair, a sense of hopelessness, which prevents any attempts to do something about one's condition. There is a sense of indifference to any further consequences, which may thus lead to reckless behaviour without consideration of right and wrong. That is the danger and defiling aspect of *atzvut*. One may be deluded to think that it is caused by being truly upset for violating Torah and a subsequent separation from G-dliness; in truth, however, it is no less than a deceptive enticement of the *yetzer hara*, man's evil disposition, that leads him astray.[18] It belongs to the realm of evil, and is synonymous with "darkness, sorrow, the nether world; it is a blemish of which it is said 'For any man that has a blemish shall not approach' (Leviticus 21:18)."[19] It is "death .. evil .. *gehenom* .."[20] "It serves no purpose at all in the service of G-d .. it reduces man to be like an inanimate rock and to despair of himself .. It is the very doorway giving access to the forces of evil.."[21]

---

17. *Tanya*, ch. 27.
18. *Tzava'at Harivash*, sect. 44 and 46; *Tanya*, ch. 26.
19. *Tikunei Zohar* 21:59a.
20. *Zohar* II:255a (cited above, note 7).
21. R. Shneur Zalman of Liadi, *Siddur im Dach*, p. 31a. *Or Hatorah*, Beshalach, p. 436; and see also *ibid.*, Tzav, p. 801.

Merirut, on the other hand, is sincere regret and contrition. The proof of sincerity lies in the fact that one does not resign himself and surrender, but will do something about it. The dispositions of *merirut* and *simchah* are not mutually exclusive in the service of G-d.[22] There remains a consciousness of truth and a pursuit of truth, and thus a vivid motivation to correct the past and to better the future. The sense of *zerizut* (alacrity and zeal), which is a distinguishing mark of *simchah*,[23] remains intact and moves to take appropriate actions. The contrite heart, and bitterness of the soul caused by its present remoteness from the light of the Divine Countenance, will not allow wallowing in self-pity. For if there is a recognition of sin and remoteness from G-dliness, there must also be a recognition and awareness of the possibility of *teshuvah*, of restoring closeness with G-d.

Thus if one really cares, if sincerely perturbed by past failures, one will not remain idle but take advantage of the opportunity to return. When lost far from home and yearning to be reunited with his loved ones, one is terribly upset about the present condition and will proportionally make

---

22. "'Serve G-d with fear, rejoice with trembling' (Psalms 2:11). What is meant by 'rejoice with trembling'? .. Where there is 'rejoicing' there should also be 'trembling'." (*Berachot* 30b; *cf. Midrash Tehilim* 100:3) On this the Baal Shem Tov comments: In the physical realm, when there is *yirah* (fear) there cannot be rejoicing, and when there is rejoicing there cannot be fear. Only in the service of G-d it is possible for both fear and love and rejoicing to co-exist simultaneously; *Keter Shem Tov*, sect. 349 (and see also *ibid.*, sect. 36 and 127). This principle is stated already in *Sifre*, Va'etchanan, beg. of sect. 32. *Cf.* also *Tzava'at Harivash*, sect. 110: "One is to serve G-d with fear and joy. These are 'two inseparable friends'."
23. *Reishit Chochmah*, Sha'ar Ho'ahavah, ch. 11 (p. 107b).

every effort to escape it. The awareness and anticipation of the happiness and joy of the homecoming motivates every conceivable effort.[24]

---

24. See "The Dynamics of Teshuvah," end of sect. VII.

III

True love of G-d and *atzvut* are mutually exclusive. On the other hand, the true love of G-d, which sometimes may lead to *merirut* (of *teshuvah*), is inseparable from the principle of *simchah*.[25] R. Eliyahu de Vidas, author of *Reishit Chochmah*, thus notes that love of G-d presupposes the acquisition of three qualities: (a) *bitachon* (trust); (b) *emunah* (faith); and (c) *simchah* (joy). These three qualities or attributes are intertwined and interdependent: Without *emunah* there cannot be *bitachon*. *Emunah* leads to *bitachon*: belief in the Creator means to realize that any success in this world or in the world-to-come comes from Him. Thus one realizes the need to trust in Him and to love Him with all one's heart. *Emunah* itself already implies that one does not fear any evil but accepts all occurrences with gladness.

---

25. See *Reishit Chochmah*, Sha'ar Ho'ahavah, end of ch. 10 (p. 105b): "*Ahavah* (Love of G-d) and *simchah* are one and the same." Cf. also R. Eleazar of Worms, *Sefer Roke'ach*, beg. s.v. Shoresh Ho'ahavah; and *Or Torah*, end of sect. 178.

R. Eliyahu offers the analogy of a servant who recognizes his master to be generous and considerate: even when the servant sees his master burdening him with hard work, he realizes that his master is really seeking to do him great favours and to exalt him.

He who believes in G-d whole-heartedly, of necessity also trusts in Him with a powerful *bitachon*, a *bitachon* that assures that one will not be afraid of anything. This *bitachon* means total peace of mind from all and anything that might cause anxiety; for there is an absorbing reliance on the One in whom we trust to be an impenetrable shield of protection against all and any harm.

In turn, *bitachon* and *emunah* must lead to *simchah*. For the servant who truly trusts in his master, and who truly believes that his service is meaningful and effective, will serve with joy. He will be happy in whatever place he is told to be, and will endure all that happens to him, just as a sick person willingly accepts bitter medicine because of his belief and trust that it will cure him. In this frame of mind one is freed from all mundane worries: for one is fully content with his lot and with whatever he has, saying, "I have sufficient with what the blessed Creator has decreed for me." *Simchah* thus is the all-inclusive attribute.[26]

---

26. *Reishit Chochmah*, Sha'ar Ho'ahavah, ch. 12. On all this see also *Shevet Mussar*, ch. 14 (and *cf*. there ch. 10: "If you see a person who is always dejected, know that it is his scanty *bitachon* that causes his *atzvut*; do not dwell in his vicinity!"); *Tanya*, ch. 26, 27, and 33; *ibid*., Igeret Hateshuvah, ch. 11, and Igeret Hakodesh, sect. XI.

IV

In real life, however, all this appears easier said than done. Intellectually it is very easy to recognize and appreciate these truisms, but very often they appear as no more than utopian theory. In practice we are forced to confront the stark realities of life, the continuous cycle of the ups and downs of our existence: physical suffering, real or imagined; spiritual frustrations; failures; worries about the unseen future; happy dreams and expectations exploding like overblown balloons; gripping anxieties; attacks of melancholy feelings, self-pity and self-depreciation when facing a reality that does not appear to hold any promise of improvement.

Sometimes such feelings are brought on by ourselves, when we reflect on the past, present and future of ourselves or even of others. At other times they strike us all on their own, seemingly beyond our control: we just feel dejected, listless, hopeless, depressed.

Very often the person filled with anxiety and melancholy thinks that this is but a personal burden, that he or she is the only one affected this way: "everyone else seems happy or has reasons for happiness, and only *my* situation is different; I alone suffer."

In fact, however, this is part of the human reality. It is part of general human psychology and can strike everyone, in all walks of life and on all planes of material or spiritual levels. But if this is the case, then it cannot be a situation that we are simply stuck with.

Torah, in all its facets, is universal, eternal, realistic. "It is not a vain thing for you, for it is your life!" (Deuteronomy 32:47) If Torah, therefore, condemns melancholy and anxiety, if Torah demands "Serve G-d with joy, come before Him with exultation" (Psalms 100:2), then Torah speaks of a reality that is always here and now, a reality that is within the reach and ability of each and everyone.[27] There must be an escape for the tormented soul to find peace of mind, to lead a healthy life of hope, meaningfulness and cheerfulness! How?

The Torah decrees: "What is the cure for those who suffer from diseases of the soul? They should go to the wise who are physicians of the soul, and they will heal their maladies by instructing them about the proper dispositions to acquire.."[28]

Anxiety, depression, melancholy, are diseases affecting

---

27. *Shemot Rabba* 34:1: "The Holy One, blessed be He, does not impose burdensome precepts upon His creatures. He comes to man according to his own strength .. according to the ability of each individual." Cf. *Avodah Zara* 3a; and see below, text relating to note 30; and "The Dynamics of Teshuvah," sect. I.
28. Rambam, *Hilchot De'ot* 2:1; *Shemonah Perakim*, ch. 3.

us today no less than ever before. Following is the prescription of one of those 'physicians of the soul': a letter by R. Menachem Mendel of Lubavitch, author of *Tzemach Tzedek*,[29] in free translation with the addition of some references and explanatory notes.

※　　※　　※

---

29. This letter appears in *Igrot Kodesh .. Admur Hatzemach Tzedek*, III:no. 4. It appears there in two versions. The translation follows the first version, except for a few emendations and insertions from the second one.

Letter of the Tzemach Tzedek

"..As for your query about anxiety .. one should definitely pray to G-d for cheerfulness, as it is said "Cause the soul of Your servant to rejoice" (Psalms 86:4), and "Remove from us grief and sighing" (*Amidah*).

Even so, fear of anxiety is sometimes brought on by oneself. In turn, one is also free and able to refrain from it. This is clearly evident from the fact that we are enjoined by a prohibition in the Torah not to be afraid and terrified when conducting warfare, as it is written "Do not be fainthearted" (Deuteronomy 20:3). *Rambam, Sefer Mitzvot Gadol, [Sefer Mitzvot Katan, and Chinuch]* count this as one of the 613 *mitzvot*. Offhand, though, this appears rather strange, for what is a person to do when overcome by fear and dread when perceiving the bloodshed of war? Commandments apply only to situations where man is free to choose to do or not to do, as explained in Rambam's *Shemonah Perakim*, chapter 2![30]

---

30. See there also ch. 8. Cf. above, note 27.

Note, however, that every soul has three 'garments': thought, speech and action.[31] These are the principal faculties relating to the actions or behaviour of man, and through these one can freely choose to think, speak or act as one pleases. It follows then that even if feelings of anxiety do arise, one is able to rid oneself of the thought, speech and actions relating to these, especially in terms of not thinking or speaking about them at all and to divert one's thought and speech to the very opposite of anxiety, as explained in *Tanya*, chapter 14.[32]

In this context we are commanded "Do not be faint-hearted;" that is, do not think about fear. Rambam thus rules in the seventh chapter of *Hilchot Melachim* (par. 15): "He who allows himself in warfare to entertain thoughts that would alarm him, violates a prohibition of the Torah."

The fact is, that as soon as one stops thinking about it altogether, the feelings of anxiety will disappear of themselves. At the very least, the anxiety will become dormant and will no longer be sensed, and after a few days it will be nullified altogether to the point of no longer arising in his mind — not even as a *machshavah zarah* (alien thought). This indeed is the meaning of "Do not be faint-hearted."

Anxiety is nullified by withdrawing our thoughts from it. For all emotions are sustained by the brain-faculty of *da'at* ('knowledge'). *Da'at* is called the "key compounding the six (emotive attributes),"[33] and is vested in the emotions by means of thought. A removal of the thought, therefore,

---

31. See *Tanya*, ch. 4 and 6.
32. See there also ch. 17-19, 25, and 44.
33. *Zohar* II:77a. See *Tanya*, ch. 3, and *ibid.*, Igeret Hakodesh, sect. XV.

will of itself remove the faculty of *da'at* from the emotion. This will then prevent that emotion from being aroused, and it simply ceases to be. (This is clearly evident from the halachic ruling stated in *Yevamot* 53b..). The *Gemara* in *Berachot* 60a also indicates that man has control over being afraid or not being afraid.[34]

The principal way of achieving a removal of *da'at* and thought from anxiety, is by making sure to divert one's thought to — and vesting it in — cheerful subjects, like the study of Torah which gladdens the heart[35]: setting daily periods for study, ideally together with another person[36] (for both *nigleh* — such as the Code of *Orach Chayim*, e.g., the laws of the blessings to be recited every morning, the laws of

---

34. That *Gemara* quotes Psalms 112:7 "He shall not be afraid of evil tidings; his heart is steadfast, trusting in G-d," of which Raba said that the first clause explains the second one, and the second one the first one: (a) "He will not fear evil tidings" — *because* "his heart is steadfast, trusting in G-d;" and (b) "His heart is steadfast, trusting in G-d" — *therefore* "he will not fear evil tidings."

    The *Gemara* relates there that R. Yishmael noticed a student who looked afraid, and said to him: "You must be a sinner, because it is written 'The sinners in Zion are afraid' (Isaiah 33:14)." Likewise, Rav Hamnuna noticed that Yehudah ben Nathan sighed, and said to him: "This man wants to bring suffering upon himself, as it is written 'For the thing which I did fear is come upon me, and that which I dreaded has overtaken me' (Job 3:25)." (*Cf.* below, note 47) Both the disciple and Yehudah protested that Scripture says 'Happy is the man who is always afraid' (Proverbs 28:14); but both were answered that this relates specifically to words of Torah: one should be afraid (i.e., concerned) lest he forget them, and thus must always review his studies. (*Cf.* below, note 45)

35. See above, note 7.
36. See *Berachot* 63b; and *Ta'anit* 7a.

the reading of the *Shema*, the laws of *tefilah*, and so forth — and *pnimiyut haTorah*, a study of *ketavim* (Chassidic discourses) and so forth). A diversion of thought may also be effected by thinking of significant and cheerful subjects of mundane matters.

Moreover, avoid discussing any subjects related to (or possibly causing) dejection, Heaven forbid. Always express yourself in a manner indicating joy, as if the heart were filled with happiness — *even if you do not really feel that way at the time.* By acting this way, one ends up that way.[37] For man is affected by his deeds and actions to the point that ultimately these will become ingrained in his heart, as stated by Rambam (*Hilchot De'ot*, end of chapter 1): "How shall man train himself in these dispositions so that they become ingrained? By frequent repetition of actions consistent with these dispositions .. and thus these dispositions will become a fixed part of his soul."

Rambam discusses this at length in the fourth chapter of *Shemonah Perakim*, the chapter dealing with "Cures for the Diseases of the Soul." This principle is stated also in *Sefer Hachinuch*,[38] and in numerous places in other sources. Though their words are not in need of any support or proof, nonetheless, one can adduce further evidence from the works of the *Kabbalah*: note carefully *Pardes Rimonim*, Sha'ar Hagevanim, chapter 1. In fact, this is supported already by the *Zohar* which states that everything depends on man's actions.[39]

In summation, then, it is imperative to guard one's

---

37. Cf. *Shevet Mussar*, ch. 28.
38. See there, sect. 16, 31, 40, 95, 99, 216, 264, 286, 299 etc.
39. *Zohar* III:92b. See there also 34b and 119a; and see note 41.

thought, speech and action. Do not allow your thoughts to dwell on matters of worry and anxiety, but speak and act as stated above. If you do so, this will ingrain cheerful dispositions in the soul, and the Almighty will pour forth from above a spirit of joy and gladness of the heart. For thus I heard from my grandfather (the *Alter Rebbe,* in the village of Piena[40]): "The Maggid interpreted the verse 'As the appearance of man above upon it' (Ezekiel 1:26): corresponding to the disposition shown by man below, he is shown from Above!"[41] (My grandfather) therefore prevented me from singing tunes with overtones of sadness in the evening-prayer (which I recited prior to his passing, with a melancholy tune), waited for me to conclude my prayer, and then told me the teaching of the Maggid.

Train yourself to prevent any form of melancholy. For man must remove from his heart every form of anxiety, even when there is cause for anxiety .. Such feelings are but an enticement of the *yetzer* (evil inclination) and must be cast off like truly alien and evil thoughts.[42] For thus we are commanded "Do not follow after your heart.." (Numbers 15:39) — which is an explicit prohibition (one of the 613 precepts of the Torah) enjoining us to divert the mind from

---

40. This is the village where the *Alter Rebbe* spent his last days and passed away.
41. The interpretation reads this verse as follows: "As the appearance of man (below, so) it is upon him from Above." See the Maggid's *Likutei Amarim,* sect. 29; *Or Torah,* sect. 134, and *ibid.,* Hossafot, par. 19 and 66. *Cf.* also *Tzava'at Harivash,* sect. 142, and the notes *ad loc.*

    Cf. Zohar II:184b: "'Serve G-d with joy' — the cheerfulness of man draws upon himself another, the Supernal cheerfulness." See also *ibid.,* 218a.
42. See above, notes 18-21.

evil thoughts of sin, as stated by Rambam (*Hilchot Avodah Zara* 2:3). In truly like manner one must divert one's thought in our context.[43]

Insofar that anxiety is sometimes viewed as a virtue, this is only in the proper context of the teaching of our sages not to convey the secrets of the Torah "except to one whose heart is anxious within him"[44] — (i.e., those who are anxious about their soul being afar from the light of the *En Sof*, blessed be He), and of this it is said, "This is my comfort in my affliction, that Your word has revived me" (Psalms 119:50).[45]"

---

43. See also *Tanya*, beg. of ch. 27.
44. *Chagigah* 13a.
45. See R. Dov Ber of Lubavitch, *Derech Chayim*, ch. 28-29; *idem.*, *Kuntres Hahitpa'alut*, pp. 59-60.

APPENDIX[46]

A

"..I am very much pained noting from your letter how much you are sometimes absorbed in worries about your health. If you will but listen to me, stay away from such worries to the utmost extreme, by total diversion of your mind from it. Trust in the mercies of G-d, and He will surely send His word and heal you. By dwelling on such worries one is actually and directly damaging oneself, both physically — as clearly evident and empirically proven — as well as spiritually..

Bitachon, trust in G-d, removes incitements and judgments, as stated in *Reishit Chochmah*, Sha'ar Ho'ahavah,

---

46. Short excerpts from additional letters of the *Tzemach Tzedek*, appearing in the same volume of *Igrot Kodesh*, nos. 5, 2, and 31 respectively.

chapter 12, commenting on "But him who trusts in G-d, He shall encompass with *chessed* (love; kindness)" (Psalms 32:10): *chessed* shall encompass him and hide him from all that would harm him, thus saving him from all worldly afflictions.[47] This reference is to the aspect of '*chessed* of *Atik Yomin*,' which is called *rav chessed* (abundant *chessed*) and radiates without any impediments and limitations,[48] that is, even if the person is not deservant at all. The essence of *bitachon* relates to this aspect of *chessed*, because it is the source of continuous Providence, as explained there (in *Reishit Chochmah*) at length."

B

"..It is most important to be cheerful at all times, for then you will be shown cheerfulness and favours from Above, as well-known, and as we heard from our master (the Alter Rebbe).."[49]

---

47. Note the interpretation of this verse in *Keter Shem Tov*, sect. 230, and *Or Torah*, sect. 212: "'But him who trusts in G-d, He will encompass with *chessed*;' on the other hand, he who is continuously afraid of the attribute of *din* (judgment) and punishment thereby attaches himself to judgments, and, Heaven forbid, evil may befall him, as it is said 'That which they dread I will bring upon them' (Isaiah 66:4; *cf.* above, note 34). For man is attached to the object of his thought (see *Tzava'at Harivash*, sect. 69, and the notes *ad loc.*; *Keter Shem Tov*, sect. 56). Thus if he thinks of *din*, he is attached to *din*. But when he trusts in the [Divine] *chessed*, he attaches his soul to it, and the *chessed* will encompass him."
48. See *Tanya*, Igeret Hakodesh, sect. X and XIII.
49. See above, text relating to note 41.

C

"..No doubt but that you have *sayata dishmaya* (special Divine assistance) because you are cheerful. My beloved friend, make them sing, for our master (the *Alter Rebbe*) said that *simchah* in the observance of *mitzvot*, and song, annul all judgments and denunciations in both spiritual and material matters.."[50]

---

50. See R. Shneur Zalman of Liadi, *Torah Or*, Va'eira, p. 57d: "Even as *simchah* above signifies the sweetening of judgments, so, too, below, in the soul of man, it nullifies all internal and external obstacles and impediments .. causing them to be repelled of themselves, just as darkness is removed by light." On *hamtakat hadinim* (the sweetening of judgments) through *simchah*, see also R. Mosheh Cordovero, *Zivchei Shelamim*, p. 18a.

On the significance of song as both motivation and verification of *simchah*, see *Zohar* II:93a; *Reishit Chochmah*, Sha'ar Ho'ahavah, ch. 10, at length (noting, among others, that "song causes *devekut* .. a cleaving of the soul to G-d;" cf. the quotation of *Livnat Hasapir*, Noach, in R. Meir ibn Gabbai, *Avodat Hakodesh*, III:ch. 10); R. Judah Halevi, *Kuzary* II:64-65, and the commentaries *Kol Yehudah* and *Otzar Nechmad, ad loc.*; and R. Eleazar Azkari, *Sefer Charedim*, Mitzvot Lo-Ta'aseh min Hatorah, end of ch. 7.

See also *Arachin* 11a: "Whence do we know from the Torah the principle for the obligation of song? .. R. Mathna said from 'Because you did not serve G-d, your G-d, with joy and gladness of the heart' (Deuteronomy 28:47). Which is the service 'with joy and gladness of the heart'? You must say it is song." (See commentary of *Maharsha, ad loc.*) (Cf. also II Kings 3:15, and *Yerushalmi, Sukah* 5:1; *Shabbat* 30b; *Zohar* I:216b.)

On song and music as a means of dispelling sadness and melancholy, see I Samuel 16:14-23; Rambam, *Shemonah Perakim*, ch. 5. Cf. Rambam, *Hilchot Yessodei Hatorah* 7:4; and *Moreh Nevuchim* III:45.

Religious Duty and
Religious Experience in Chassidism

Religious Duty and Religious Experience in Chassidism

Table of Contents

I	The Dilemma	155
II	Torah and *Mitzvot*: Basis for All	158
III	*Lishmah*	163
IV	Deed and Thought	166
V	The Study of Torah	170
VI	Two Levels	174
VII	Primacy of Torah-Study	176

Religious Duty and Religious Experience in Chassidism

I

The Dilemma

Mystical movements invariably stress the mystical experience. It is an experience of all-pervading ecstasy: sensing a reality different from that of our every-day life. It means penetrating beyond the world that appears to our physical senses and being absorbed in a higher, spiritual realm. This spiritual realm is regarded as true and real. The awareness and experience of it is seen as an ultimate goal. Man is to experience, to be aware of, and to be gripped by, the true and real, as opposed to being confounded by the transient — and thus misleading — world of appearance.

This goal, however, can be achieved only by transcending the confinements of time and space: by a profound concentration on the Absolute immanent throughout, albeit hidden and concealed. Mysticism thus demands purity of intent (*kavanah*). All one's doings must be ordered in such a way that they are not performed by rote, mechanical or habitual. They require an intense devotion that places all actions into the full context of the all-pervasive reality of the Absolute. Perfunctory motions, ego-centric pursuits, self-concern in any shape or manner, have no place in this scheme. Self-effacement (*bitul hayesh*) is the prerequisite major premise, and pure awe and love of the Divine are the means, to achieve the ideal.

This poses a serious problem. What is one to do when enjoined to fulfill specific religious duties, when subject to an objective code of laws, as mandated by Torah and *mitzvot*? It would seem that tensions must arise between the legal obligation to perform rituals on the one hand, and the ideal condition of the religious experience on the other. What is one to do if there is a duty (*mitzvah*) to be performed in a set time and place, when one is not in the proper frame of mind to do so in ideal fashion of right intent and devotion? Which of the two takes precedence — the physical act or the mental-emotional consideration?

This problem is quite serious. It would seem to affect Chassidism in a very special way. For Chassidism is emphatic in its insistence to inculcate the principle of the "ideal action." It insists that our life and actions, particularly with respect to Torah and *mitzvot*, be imbued with the right intent and proper devotion: with *ahavah veyirah* (love and awe); *lishmah* — *leshem Hashem* (for the good deed's own sake — for the sake of G-d).

Paradoxically, this very problem is at the root of the secular-popular stereotype distortion of Chassidism. In this misinterpretation, Chassidism is presented as careless or negligent in matters of *Halachah*, or as an emotional reaction and sentimental rebellion against the formal 'rigors' of *Halachah* and 'Rabbinic legalism.'

In other words, Chassidism is depicted as having surrendered Halachic duties for the sake of the mystical experience. Formal ritual is said to have been sacrificed for the sake of emotive awareness, the objective act yielded for the sake of subjective feeling. This view of Chassidism, however, is based on total ignorance. Those who present it betray their failure to study or understand the teachings and practices of Chassidism. Obviously they did not take the trouble of studying, at the very least, the basic, seminal teachings and practices of the first leaders and guides of Chassidism, namely R. Israel Baal Shem Tov and R. Dov Ber, the Maggid of Mezhirech. Even a cursory glance at their teachings would have shown how totally wrong and distorted these views are.

Chassidism itself was fully aware of the problem. Its leaders dealt with it quite explicitly and in no uncertain terms. In the pages following we shall see how R. Dov Ber of Mezhirech, disciple and successor of the Baal Shem Tov, dealt with this question.*

---

* Unless stated otherwise, the quotations are taken from the Maggid's teachings in the following works: *MDL* (*Maggid Devarav Leya'akov*, also called *Likutei Amarim*), ed. Kehot: New York 1984; *OrTo* (*Or Torah*), ed. Kehot: New York 1984; *LiYek* (*Likutim Yekarim*), ed. Toldot Aharon: Jerusalem 1974; *OrEm* (*Or HaEmet*), ed. Husziatin: New York 1960; *TzHar* (*Tzava'at Harivash*), ed. Kehot: New York 1982. All other sources are spelled out fully.

II

Torah and *Mitzvot*: Basis for All

The Midrash defines the purpose of this world's creation with the words, "The Holy One, blessed be He, desired to have an abode in the lower worlds."[1] Thus it is man's task to establish an abode for Divinity in the terrestrial realm.

Man is to manifest G-d's immanence in the physical world. The achievement of this manifestation establishes the ultimate unity of G-d, that is, that G-d is recognized to be the sole true reality. To that end man was given the Torah, the revelation of the Divine precepts which instruct[2] man precisely "the way in which he is to walk and the deed he is to do."[3]

---

1. *Tanchuma*, Nasso:16. See there also Bechukotai:3; and *Bamidbar Rabba* 13:6. Cf. MDL, Hossafot, par. 37.
2. See below, note 32.
3. See Exodus 18:20.

Torah is the intermediary between man and the world and the Divine. Creation comes about through Torah.[4] The world is sustained through Torah: the very existence of the universe and all therein, man's every need, all man has and receives, depend on the Torah.[5] The Torah thus is the direct link between the upper and the lower, between G-d and man, in both directions: it is the channel through which the supernal effusions and emanations flow downward to sustain all beings, and it is the channel through which man attaches himself to the Divine.[6]

"The Torah and the Holy One, blessed be He, are altogether one."[7] On this Zoharic maxim, the Maggid comments: Divinity *per se* is beyond any creature's grasp and endurance.[8] The Almighty, therefore, 'condensed' and 'concentrated' Himself (*tzimtzum*),[9] as it were, into the letters of the Torah.[10] With these letters He then created the world, as it is said, "The Holy One, blessed be He, created the world by means of the Torah."[11] This refers to the 'Ten Fiats of Creation' in the very first chapter of the Torah.[12]

---

4. *Tanchuma*, Bereishit:1; *Bereishit Rabba* 1:1; *Zohar* I:5a, and 47a. See also below, note 11.
5. *Zohar* I:47a. See *Pesachim* 68b. *Tanchuma*, Bereishit:1. *Pirkei deR. Eliezer*, ch. 16.
6. *OrTo*, par. 105. *LiYek*, par. 131.
7. See *Zohar* II:90b. See also *ibid*. I:24a, and II:60a.
8. See *Tikunei Zohar* 17a; and *cf. Tanya*, ch. 4.
9. For a detailed explanation of the concept of *tzimtzum*, see *Mystical Concepts in Chassidism*, ch. II.
10. For a detailed explanation of the significance of the *aleph-bet*, the letters of the Torah, see my "Gimatriya: The Principle of Numerical Interpretation."
11. *Zohar* II:204a. See *Sefer Yetzirah* 2:2; *Berachot* 55a; Rashi on Job 28:23.
12. *Avot* 5:1. *Rosh Hashanah* 32a.

The letters of the Torah dim and conceal the essence of Divinity. Nonetheless, they do not become a separate entity but remain fully unified with G-d. G-d is not separate or distinct from Torah, as it is said, "He and His causations are one."[13] On the other hand, the Torah speaks to man. Thus we are able to relate to it. By virtue of the Torah's identification with G-d, therefore, the letters of the Torah enable us to absorb and endure G-dliness. Whatever apprehension of, and attachment to, the Divine, that man may achieve, is possible only by means of the Torah and its *mitzvot*.[14]

In this vein, the Maggid interprets the term כביכול. This term is usually found in context of an anthropomorphic analogy, and is generally translated 'as it were,' or 'if it were possible to say so.'[15] The Maggid reads it as a compound of two words: כ"ב and יכול. The implication is that G-d concentrated Himself into the כ"ב — 22 — letters of the Torah's alphabet, and thereby יכול — *it is possible* for G-d to be in this world.[16]

The Torah is thus "G-d's 'garment'" which makes it possible for a finite creation to come into being and for the infinite G-d to dwell within it.[17]

Any indwelling of the *Shechinah* and Divine emana-

---

13. *Tikunei Zohar* 3b.
14. *MDL*, par. 177; *OrTo*, par. 248. See also *MDL*, par. 164; *OrTo*, par. 200.
15. See Rashi on *Yoma* 3b, and on *Megilah* 21a, s.v. *kibeyachol*.
16. *No'am Elimelech*, Vayera, on Genesis 18:1. — Cf. *Shenei Luchot Haberit*, Torah Shebe'al Peh, s.v. *kibeyachol*; *Techilat Chochmah* III:1, klal 35; and *Pachad Yitzchak*, s.v. *kibeyachol*.
17. *OrTo*, par. 167. *TzHar*, par. 111, and see there for further references.

tions requires a 'receptacle,' something to have a 'hold' on these, something to which they may become attached.[18] For the holiness of a Divine emanation is too bright and intense to be absorbed as it is in itself by man and the world. Thus there is need for a medium through which it may vest itself below.[19] This medium is Torah and *mitzvot*.[20]

Thus it is said, "The Holy One, blessed be He, desired *lezakot* the people of Israel, and therefore He gave them Torah and *mitzvot* in abundance."[21] The term *lezakot* means to refine and purify. The implication is that there is a refinement and purification of Israel's material reality so that it will be able to become attached and joined to holiness. This is indeed suggested by the term *mitzvah-mitzvot*, which is an idiom of *tzavta* — attachment, union.[22] This principle is alluded in the saying of "A *mitzvah* brings about a *mitzvah*"[23]: doing a *mitzvah* brings about, and leads to, *tzavta* — attachment and conjunction, while "An *aveirah* (transgression) brings about an *aveirah*,"[24] i.e., overstepping, to pass beyond, and to be separated from the Creator.[25]

By means of Torah and *mitzvot*, therefore, man — the

---

18. *Zohar* I:88a. Cf. *OrTo*, par. 491; *LiYek*, par. 111. See also *Zohar* III:187a; and *Tanya*, ch. 35 and end of ch. 53.
19. *MDL*, par. 259; *OrTo*, par. 363.
20. *MDL*, par. 179. *OrTo*, par. 71, 80, and 245.
21. *Makot* 23b.
22. See *Sefer Chareidim*, Teshuvah, ch. 7; *Or Hachayim* on Numbers 27:23; R. Shneur Zalman of Liadi, *Likutei Torah*, Bechukotai, p. 45c; *Sefer Halikutim-Dach*, s.v. mitzvah, p. 1089*ff.*; *Likutei Sichot*, vol. VII, p. 30*ff. Hayom Yom*, p. 102.
23. *Avot* 4:2.
24. *Ibid.*
25. *MDL*, par. 259; *OrTo*, par. 363.

prospective recipient — renders himself into a proper receptacle. Thus he becomes like a channel or conduit for the supernal 'spring' from which the beneficent abundance flows forth to that individual and to the whole world.[26]

In this context, too, the Torah is said to consist solely of Divine Names.[27] The Divine Names are in effect synonymous with the Divine Attributes.[28] Thus all the words and aspects of the Torah are, or signify, the Divine Attributes. Hence, as certain parts of the Torah are studied or observed, the corresponding Attributes are aroused to become manifest below. When one is called by name, one leaves everything aside to answer the caller. So, too, G-d, who is 'concentrated' in the Torah (His Names — Attributes), and altogether one with His Name, responds to the one that calls Him through His Torah.[29]

---

26. *OrTo*, par. 105; *LiYek*, par. 131. See also *MDL*, par. 94, and *OrTo*, par. 243.
27. *Zohar* II:90b and 124a. Ramban, Intr. to his Torah-Commentary, and *idem, Torat Hashem Temimah*, (*Kitvei Ramban*, vol. I:p. 167f). Cf. *MDL*, par. 84, 177, 214, and 223; *OrTo*, par. 65, 152, and 248.
28. See *Zohar* II:42b, and III:288a. Cf. *Mystical Concepts in Chassidism*, p. 59f. and notes 203 there.
29. *OrEm*, p. 15a. Cf. *Eliyahu Rabba*, ch. 18; *Yalkut Shimoni*, Eicha, par. 1034.

III

Lishmah

The intimate and inseparable relationship between Torah and the very existence and sustenance of all beings thus appears quite clearly. In this context of the Torah's cosmic significance it is readily seen why the Maggid emphasizes that when learning Torah one must keep in mind the Talmudic saying, "The Holy One, blessed be He, has in His world only the four cubits of *Halachah*."[30] Thus one should say in his heart: "His blessed Being is concentrated, and dwells, here (in Torah); hence it is only fit to study Torah with joy, with awe and with love."[31]

In other words, Torah and *mitzvot* must be studied and fulfilled *lishmah*, which means: (a) *For its name*, i.e., as its

---

30. *Berachot* 8a.
31. *OrEm*, p. 15a. *TzHar*, par. 119.

very name indicates — the term 'Torah' meaning 'instruction, teaching,'[32] for it teaches man the way in which he is to walk and instructs him in the awe and love of G-d.[33] (b) *For its sake*, לשמה — i.e., לשם ה' for the sake of G-d[34]: to bring about a realization of the Divine purpose, to cause the Divine 'delight,' as it were, from G-d having commanded and His will having been fulfilled.[35]

In turn, this implies that man learn Torah and practice *mitzvot* with fervor and ardor (*hitlahavut*). For one could conceivably study Torah as a natural act, simply because of enjoying the study, just as one may indulge in business or other mundane affairs simply because one enjoys doing so. In essence, then, these two actions are not distinguishable from one another! The principal Divine 'delight' in man's performance of *mitzvot*, therefore, is not from the very act itself, but from the extent of man's *hitlahavut*, from the devotional involvement, the sense of *lishmah*.[36]

We note here the emphasis on *kavanah* (intention; motivation; devotion), the significance of *lishmah*, the requirement of *ahavah veyirah*, as indispensable ingredients for the religious act. This reiterates the Zoharic maxim that *ahavah* and *yirah* are the wings needed for Torah and *mitzvot* to soar upwards to effect their ultimate purpose.[37]

The Maggid, as do Kabbalah and Chassidut in general,

---

32. *Zohar* III:53b. See also *ibid.*, III:260a. *Netivot Olam*, Netiv Hatorah, ch. 1, and Netiv Ha'emunah, ch. 2.
33. *OrTo*, par. 317, and 453; *LiYek*, par. 201. *Cf. MDL*, par. 122.
34. *OrTo*, par. 317, and 419. *Cf. Sha'ar Hamitzvot*, Va'etchanan, and *Sha'ar Ma'amarei Razal*, Avot VI.
35. *MDL*, par. 134.
36. *Ibid.*
37. *Tikunei Zohar* 10:25b.

never tires of stressing this requirement.[38] Our initial problem thus comes to the fore: what is man to do if and when he lacks this emotive condition, if and when — due to his mundane entanglements — he has difficulty in bringing himself to the ideal state of *ahavah* and *yirah*? If the state of *hitlahavut* is the ultimate achievement, would it not follow that perhaps man should expend all his efforts to achieve just that, to achieve the inner, spiritual perfection, as opposed to the external, corporeal action of the study of Torah and the practice of *mitzvot*?

---

38. See *MDL*, par. 60, 64, 246, and 253. *OrTo*, par. 105, 108, 341 and 498.

IV

Deed and Thought

The Maggid was quite aware of this tension. His essential answer may be put as follows:

Kavanah, lishmah, hitlahavut, are the ideal state. Nonetheless, the study of Torah and the practice of *mitzvot* have an objective validity of their own. Thus they must be followed even if the ideal state has not been attained yet. One cannot possibly achieve *yirah*, the fear and awe of G-d, without a prior absolute and objective fulfillment of Torah and *mitzvot*![39] *Hitlahavut* is not realizable except by way of actions: by way of deeds to which it can attach itself and in which it becomes vested.[40]

Indeed, *hitlahavut* in isolation harbors an element of

---

39. *Kedushat Levi*, Lech Lecha, on Genesis 15:8.
40. *MDL*, par. 134.

danger. For he who acts purely out of love, from a sense of immense ardor and ecstasy (*hitlahavut*), may get carried away and fail to be meticulous with his obligations. *Hitlahavut* thus need be tempered and restrained by a sense of fear, submission and discipline.[41]

When the Maggid states that it is impossible to achieve *devekut* (attachment to G-d) except by means of Torah and *mitzvot*, he is quite explicit in stating that he means the *act* of Torah and *mitzvot*. For *mitzvot* have three aspects: thought, speech, and deed. When the Torah was given at Sinai, it was given by way of *speech* (G-d's words in the proclamation of the commandments). Needless to say that this includes *thought* as well, because speech derives from thought. The Torah was thus given by way of thought and speech, and the *deed* was left to us. Hence, when we actually perform *mitzvot*, in actual deed, we effect the unity of the *act* of the *mitzvah* with its *thought* and *speech*.[42]

Let us take, for example, the *mitzvah* of *tefillin*. The section in the Torah which ordains the *mitzvah* of *tefillin* is the *speech* of the *mitzvah*. The *kavanah* is the *thought*. The commandment itself is the *deed*. That is why our sages said, "He who recites the *Shema* without *tefillin* bears false witness against himself."[43] For how can the *thought* (the *kavanah*) vest itself in the *speech*? What will the thought and speech dwell upon if not on the actual deed? If, again, he recites the *Shema* with *tefillin*, the speech becomes a garment unto the thought, and the deed becomes a garment unto the speech.[44]

---

41. OrTo, par. 124.
42. MDL, par. 179; OrTo, par. 72, and 80.
43. *Berachot* 14b.
44. OrTo, par. 245.

Thus despite the inestimable importance of *kavanah*, the very act of the *mitzvah* has an objective, independent value and validity of its own. It may not be suspended, therefore, even when the proper *kavanah* is lacking.

The Maggid lays down what he calls "an important rule": When a *mitzvah* comes to man's mind, he should not refrain from doing it because of his apprehensions that its performance may cause in him a feeling of pride or self-satisfaction, or whatever other ulterior motive. One must pursue the *mitzvah* anyway. No doubt but that from the present lack of *lishmah* he will eventually come to a state of *lishmah*.[45] The good deed in and by itself effects a 'good instrument' (the 'body' of the deed), while the faculty of thought (*kavanah*) effects the *pnimiyut* (inwardness; the 'soul') of that instrument.[46]

For all of Torah and the *mitzvot* have an external aspect (*chitzoniyut*) which 'guards the fruit,' i.e., the inner essence (*pnimiyut*). This is analogous to the sac of the fetus and the placenta, the 'external aspects' without which the fetus cannot develop. For example, the *mitzvah* of *teshuvah* (repentance; return to G-d) has an external aspect of being motivated by fear of negative consequences.

We see this in the case of "Pharaoh *hikriv*"[47] — which our sages read to mean not only that "Pharaoh *came* close" but also that "Pharaoh *brought* close:" he brought Israel close to G-d. Pharaoh's pursuit caused Israel to do *teshuvah*.[48] Now surely Pharaoh did not intend to bring

---

45. *Pesachim* 50b.
46. *MDL*, par. 190. *TzHar*, par. 126, and see the notes there.
47. Exodus 14:10.
48. *Shemot Rabba* 21:5.

them to *teshuvah*. They did so because they feared him. Their initial motivation, therefore, was one of fear. That fear was like a shell that protects the fruit. Thereafter, however, the Israelites found the 'fruit' itself, 'ate' it and did *teshuvah* in proper fashion. Thus from the initial *shelo lishmah* (lack of *lishmah*) will ultimately come about a state of *lishmah*.[49]

---

49. *MDL*, par. 242; *OrTo*, par. 492.

V

The Study of Torah

In view of the paramount importance of *ma'aseh hamitzvot* (the actual deed or action of the *mitzvot*), the Maggid stresses the significance of studying *Halachah* in particular: "The *yetzer hara* (inclination to evil) does not seek to entice man to refrain from learning altogether, for man would not normally agree to this. Rather, the *yetzer hara* entices him not to study those subjects which will inspire *yirat Shamayim* (fear and awe of G-d), such as *Mussar* (ethical works), or *Shulchan Aruch* (Code of Jewish Law) from which one gains clear knowledge of the laws!"[50]

This is not to say that one should study only practical *Halachah* and inspirational literature like *Mussar*. Nor, for that matter, does it mean that one should concentrate on

---

50. *OrTo*, par. 22; *LiYek*, par. 237. *TzHar*, par. 117.

pnimiyut haTorah (the esoteric, inner meanings — as distinguished from *peshat*, the exoteric, outer or plain meaning — of the Torah). *Peshat* is no less than the very key necessary to enter and attain the inner part.[51]

In fact, the 'Oral Torah' (Talmud; the Rabbinic tradition explicating the 'Written Torah') is referred to as *kishutei kalah* (bridal ornaments).[52] This means that the Rabbinic analysis and discussions, in which each one expresses his insight and opinion, is analogous to each one saying, 'this or that way is a nicer ornament, this or that way is more fitting and beautiful.'[53]

The Maggid offers the following parable: A king was lost. He wandered about like an ordinary peasant in shabby clothes, and no one recognized him. When his faithful subjects finally did find and recognize him, they decided to make for him beautiful new garments. Then they started to argue among themselves: one says, '*This* will be more fitting and beautiful,' while another claims, 'No, *this* will be more fitting and beautiful.' The king is greatly delighted by these arguments, even by suggestions that are altogether inappropriate, because his subjects sincerely seek to enhance his honor and glory. In that sense, then, *pilpul*, the Oral Torah, is referred to as the 'bridal adornments.' For G-d takes delight, as it were, even from one who may arrive at a mistaken conclusion, insofar that he seeks to enhance His blessed honor.[54]

The Heavenly interrogation (after man leaves this

---

51. OrTo, par. 258. Cf. Zohar I:154a.
52. *Zohar Chadash*, Shir: 64a.
53. *MDL*, par. 88; OrTo, par. 397.
54. OrTo, par. 397.

world), "Did you conduct your business in good faith? Did you set aside times for the study of Torah?,"[55] the Maggid interprets as follows[56]: "When you conducted your business, did you do so in good faith, that is, did you think of G-d at all times, every moment, without separating your thoughts from His blessed Being? If you reply, 'But there is a *yetzer hara*!,' then you are asked: Did you set aside times for the study of Torah, for 'I have created the *yetzer hara*, but I have also created the Torah as an antidote to it[57]!'"

The Maggid elaborates on the antidotal quality of the Torah: It is written, "All that are thirsty go to the *water*"[58] — that is, go to the Torah which is referred to as water.[59] Elsewhere, though, it is written, "My word is like *fire*!"[60] There are, however, two forms of *yetzer hara*: one inflames man to commit sin, while the other cools man and casts upon him a sluggishness not to fulfill the commandments. Thus it is said, "I have created the *yetzer hara*, but I have also created the Torah as an antidote to it": with regards to the *yetzer hara* which inflames it is said, "All that are thirsty go to the water;" and with regards to the *yetzer hara* that cools and generates coldness it is said, "My word is like fire."[61]

When at times man's heart becomes 'coarse' (lit., 'material,' that is, insensitive to spirituality), the way to correct this is by attaching oneself to Torah, and thereby one will slay his evil inclination.[62] Likewise, when contrite for

---

55. *Shabbat* 31a.
56. *MDL*, par. 79; *OrTo*, par. 401.
57. *Kidushin* 30b.
58. Isaiah 55:1.
59. *Baba Kama* 17a.
60. Jeremiah 23:29.
61. *Zichron Zot*, Parshat Zachor.
62. *OrTo*, par. 84b.

having gone astray and committing sins, the study of Torah will rectify man's perverted actions.[63]

The study of Torah is so important in the teachings of the Maggid as an objective act and duty on its own, that he counts the failure to study among the most serious roots of evil. He refers to the Mishnah[64] which enumerates the four principal categories of culpable harm on the physical level, and reads these as signifying also the four principal categories of culpable harm on the spiritual level. Thus he interprets the second one — *bor*: the term *bor* means a pit, but it means also emptiness, waste, signifying a neglected and uncultivated field that was not plowed or sown.[65] In its inner sense, then, this refers to one who failed to study Torah.[66]

Rather than fasting and mortifying oneself, one should use the energy expended thereon for the study of Torah with all one's might and devotion, and thus one will ascend on the ladder of spirituality.[67] Intense study of Torah, to the point of discovering new insights (*chidushei Torah*) in Talmud and *Halachah*, purifies man for the service of G-d.[68] Moreover, as G-d and the Torah are essentially one, by binding oneself to the letters of Torah one is able to transcend the temporal.[69]

---

63. *MDL*, par. 223.
64. *Baba Kama* 2a.
65. See *Baba Metzia* 104a.
66. *OrTo*, par. 460. *TzHar*, par. 121, and see the notes there.
67. *OrTo*, par. 205d; *LiYek*, par. 178.
68. *Darkei Tzedek*, V:p. 18a.
69. *MDL*, par. 122. See there also par. 179; and *OrTo*, par. 72 (80).

VI

Two Levels

These teachings of the Maggid, essential to — and typical of — authentic Chassidism (as evident from their sources), are merely a sample, a few selected passages. They are supplemented, and vastly elaborated upon, in the wide range of his other teachings available to us.

It follows, then, quite clearly, that Chassidism must be understood to speak of two levels in man's worship of G-d:

a) There is an initial stage, relating to everyone without exception. It impresses upon man his Divinely ordained obligations to study Torah and practice *mitzvot* in accordance with all specifications of *Halachah* — as an *objective and absolute reality in itself*.

Even so, one is not to say that being occupied with G-d's Torah and *mitzvot* is in any case adequate and sufficiently holy on its own. The fact of their intrinsic and comprehensive sanctity does not negate the need for proper *kavanah*. On the contrary: the very fact of intrinsic sanctity demands the more adequate *kavanah*, pure thought and perfect speech, so that every word coming from your mouth, every single letter as well as its vowels and accents, be distinct.[70] Thus —

b) on a second, higher level, man must strive to study Torah and practice *mitzvot* in *ideal fashion*, with proper devotion and intent, with a sense of *ahavah* and *yirah*, *hitlahavut* and *devekut*.

The religious experience, therefore, the very soul and spirit of the *mitzvot*, the mystical involvement, is all-important. Nonetheless, it needs be attached to actual deeds.

The Torah enjoins us to cleave unto G-d (*devekut*). A permanent state of perfect *devekut* or *hitlahavut*, however, is humanly impossible in itself and by itself. The fulfillment of this commandment, therefore, is as our sages interpreted it: "How is it possible to cleave unto the Holy One, blessed be He, when it has been said, 'For G-d, your G-d, is a devouring fire'[71]? But this precept means, 'cleave unto His attributes: as He is compassionate, so you be compassionate...'."[72] In other words, in order to cleave unto G-d one must practice Torah and *mitzvot*.[73]

---

70. *OrTo*, par. 178; *LiYek*, par. 132.
71. Deuteronomy 4:22.
72. *Sifre*, Ekev, par. 49; *Ketuvot* 111b. See *Shabbat* 133b; and *Sotah* 14a.
73. *OrTo*, par. 167. *TzHar*, par. 111, and see the notes there.

VII

Primacy of Torah-Study

One can read a succinct summary of the above in the following guideline:

When studying Torah [or performing a *mitzvah*] one should pause every so often in order to attach oneself to His blessed Being. At the very time of actual learning, the necessary requirement of full mental involvement and concentration precludes a simultaneous pursuit of *devekut*. Nonetheless, one must still learn, for the Torah itself clears and furbishes the soul and is "A Tree of Life unto those that hold on to it."[74] In fact, if one does not learn, his *devekut* would have to cease [for "a *boor* (a boor; an empty person) cannot be fearful of sin, nor can an *am ha'aretz* (an unlearned person; an ignoramus) be scrupulously

---

74. Proverbs 3:18.

pious"⁷⁵].. Thus one must pursue Torah-study, notwithstanding the fact of the temporary suspension of *devekut* at the time of concentrating on the learning. Even so, every so often one should pause to dwell on, and reinforce, attachment to the Creator.⁷⁶

In a parallel-passage of this teaching,⁷⁷ it is expanded and elaborated on with the following words:

"If one were to sit idle, the *yetzer* (*hara*) would lead him to improper thoughts, evil desires and idle talk, and to all the other 'forces and hosts' (of the *yetzer hara*).⁷⁸ For the faculty of thought is continuously at work and never rests⁷⁹ .. Would that we, in our generations, could cleave unto the blessed Creator during the daily three prayers and the recitation of the benedictions! Thus if one were to cease studying, one would remain 'bald from here and bald from there' (i.e., forfeiting both the study of Torah and the *devekut*)."

In short, one must submit to the Divine Will expressed in Torah and *mitzvot*. One must obey it to the best of one's abilities without introducing any personal considerations, even if they appear noble and spiritual. Man's concern must be G-d-centered, and not self-centered. When all actions are geared toward fulfilling the Divine Will and 'gratification,' they become infused with G-dliness. This will also effect the ultimate goal of a Divine indwelling.⁸⁰

---

75. *Avot* 2:5.
76. *OrEm*, p. 99a. *TzHar*, par. 29.
77. Cited in margin of *TzHar*, par. 29, and see the notes there. See also *TzHar*, par. 30.
78. Cf. *Ketuvot* 59b. *Midrash Le'olam*, end of ch. 10.
79. See *MDL*, par. 176, and 252. *OrTo*, par. 118, and 179b.
80. *MDL*, par. 134.

Lamplighters:
The Philosophy of
Lubavitch Activism

Lamplighters:
The Philosophy of Lubavitch Activism

Table of Contents

Introduction	....	183
I	The Threefold Cord	186
II	Spiritual Charity	190
III	Divine Providence	192
IV	What is a *Chassid?*	196
V	Offensive vs. Defensive	199
VI	"Words from the heart enter the heart" ...	204
VII	The *Rebbe*: Soul-Geologist	209

Lamplighters: The Philosophy of Lubavitch Activism

Introduction

Over the past few decades Chabad-Lubavitch has become well-known in Jewish communities throughout the world for its intense offensive toward greater observance of Torah and *mitzvot*. Numerous young men and women move to dozens of cities and countries, often far away from their own places of origin, on *shlichut* (mission) to establish new, or fortify existing, educational institutions and to fill responsible positions involving spiritual, educational and social needs. Their sole objective is to strengthen Jewish identity and religious consciousness in their new surroundings. Many more, holding a variety of positions over the whole spectrum of professional occupations, seek, each in his or her own way, to achieve the same objective in their different environments.

A profound spirit of activism pervades the whole community of Lubavitch, involving directly or indirectly every one of its members. Thousands of Jews from every kind of background have thus been exposed to an experience and influence of classical Judaism, causing them to reorient their lives toward their historical identity and traditional values. Many of those who found the way back to their roots are now themselves active in the frontlines guiding others back.

Lubavitch seems to be an anachronism in this day and age. As early as a century ago, professional historians and sociologists, wrapped up in their statistical data and natural laws of causality, wrote off Chassidism as a passing relic and idiosyncrasy of an age long past. It seems, though, that no one informed the Chassidim of these prognostications. They defy and frustrate the prophets of doom by their tenacious, continuing survival. Verily, even after the horrible, decimating tragedy of the Holocaust which, proportionally, struck the adherents of Chassidism more than others, Chassidism today enjoys a miraculous renaissance which staggers the imagination. Like the *chol*, the legendary phoenix-bird which constantly rises again in youthful freshness from its own ashes, Chassidism blossoms again, vibrantly alive and consistently spreading.

Many wonder: whence this strength? Whence their super-human courage? Whence this unbelievable steadfastness in an age of counter-culture? In the midst of this very world Lubavitch not only stands its own ground but successfully broadens it.

The following pages are an attempt to formulate, more or less systematically, the philosophy of Lubavitch activism which inspires the Chassid to pursue his ideals unaffected by his environment. It is based on the writings and talks of the present Lubavitcher Rebbe, R. Menachem M. Schneerson *shelita*. Most of the quotations are freely translated and adapted from the original Hebrew or Yiddish. In these sources we shall seek the answers, and their rationale, to the general questions of

> 1. *What is a Chassid?* 2. *What is the Chassid's mission?* 3. *How is he to go about realizing this mission in the context of Lubavitch activism?* 4. *What is the role of the Rebbe in all this?*

More specific questions, like what is the rationale behind the Chassidic principle of disseminating the mystical lore of Chassidic teachings, and what is the basic concept of a Rebbe *per se*, are beyond the present frame of reference.* In the ultimate sense, these two aspects are intimately related with the present topic, to the point of unity; nonetheless, we shall deal here only with the exoteric face of Lubavitch rather than with the esoteric one.

---

* These subjects are dealt with in the first volume of this series ("On the Study and Propagation of *Pnimiyut HaTorah*") and in this volume ("The *Rebbe-Tzaddik* Concept in Chassidism").

I

The Threefold Cord

The foundation-stone of Chassidism is the Zoharic dictum of the intrinsic unity of G-d, Torah and Israel.[1] R. Israel Baal Shem Tov thus taught: The essence of *avodah* (worship) is that man bring himself to an all-encompassing love of G-d, love of Torah, and love of Israel.[2] And the very first declaration the Rebbe issued on the day he assumed Chassidic leadership was to the effect that these three loves are wholly and inextricably one:

> One cannot distinguish between them, for they are truly one, like unto one essence. The Baal Shem Tov states in the name of earlier sages that when seizing

---

1. *Zohar* III:73a. Cf. *Tikunei Zohar* 21:60b.
2. *Butzina Dinehura*; cited in the anthology *Sefer Baal Shem Tov*, Mishpatim, par. 17.

but a part of *etzem* (essence) one seizes it in its totality.³ Hence, as the three loves are essentially one, every one of them compounds all three; for when seizing a part of essence one seizes it all.

Where there is love of G-d but no love for Torah and Israel, that love of G-d is clearly defective.⁴ In turn, where there is a true love of Israel, then, notwithstanding the fact that this itself is one of the 'rational commandments' which reason itself obligates,⁵ ultimately one will arrive at love of Torah and G-d.

And this must be made known: a Jew who has love of G-d but lacks love of Torah or Israel is to be told and made to realize that it cannot endure. In turn, a Jew who has but love of Israel must be brought to love of Torah and love of G-d. One must further see to it that his love of Israel should not be limited to merely providing food for the hungry and water for the thirsty. *Ahavat Yisrael* (Love of Israel) also means to bring fellow-Jews to love of Torah and love of G-d.

When these three loves are united they form the

---

3. *Keter Shem Tov*, Hossafot, par. 116. See *Toldot Ya'akov Yosef*, Yitro:VI (*Keter Shem Tov*, sect. 250, and see there my notes; *Sefer Baal Shem Tov*, Nasso, par. 4). Cf. *Toldot Ya'akov Yosef*, Chaye:III, where this maxim is cited in context of the *mitzvah* of *ahavat Yisrael*, and see *Likutei Sichot*, vol. II, p. 435.
4. See *Mechilta* on Exodus 15:7; *Sifre* on Numbers 10:35; *Pesikta Rabaty*, Ki Tissa (ed. Friedmann, p. 39b). The Baal Shem Tov thus taught: "Love of Israel is love of G-d. 'You are the children of G-d, your G-d,' (Deuteronomy. 14:1) — when one loves the Father one loves the children;" *Keter Shem Tov*, Hossafot, par. 89. See "The Dynamics of *Ahavat Yisrael*," sect. VIII and XI.
5. See *Yoma* 67b. R. Saadiah Gaon, *Emunot Vede'ot* III:1*ff*.

"three-ply cord that is not quickly severed" (Ecclesiastes 4:12). That will also bring about the ultimate redemption. For just as this last *galut* (exile) was caused by the opposite of *ahavat Yisrael*,[6] so *ahavat Yisrael* will bring about the redemption from this *galut* speedily in our days.[7]

The Baal Shem Tov interpreted the Mishnah, "Torah that is not combined with work, will ultimately cease"[8]: in order for Torah to endure, it must be combined with 'work' and effort in *ahavat Yisrael*.[9] Every one must make an effort with *ahavat Yisrael* to influence a fellow-Jew to improve. Indeed, this will be to his own benefit as well, as our sages comment[10] on the verses "The poor man and the man of substance meet together, G-d enlightens the eyes of both" (Proverbs 29:13), and "The rich and the poor meet together, G-d is the Maker of them all" (Proverbs 22:2). For just as it is with those who are poor and rich in the material sense, so, too, it is with the poor and rich in the spiritual realm: when the rich benefits the poor, the Almighty benefits the rich as well.[11]

Only he who submits with complete self-sacrifice to

---

6. *Yoma* 9b. *Zohar Chadash*, Vayeshev:29d.
7. *Likutei Sichot*, II: p. 499ff. Cf. also *ibid.*, pp. 298 and 300. See "The Dynamics of *Ahavat Yisrael*," Conclusion.
8. *Avot* 2:2.
9. *Keter Shem Tov*, Hossafot, par. 86. Cf. *Yevamot* 105a and 109b: He who says that he has nothing but Torah, he has not even Torah. One must be engaged with Torah and the performance of kindness.
10. See *Temurah* 16a.
11. *Likutei Sichot* I: p. 260 (Kedoshim, sect. XV-XVI). Cf. *ibid.*, p. 134 (Bo, sect. XVII).

ahavat Yisrael can be sure of himself: he himself will remain intact, and he will also be able to restore the spiritual losses of others.[12] R. Shneur Zalman of Liadi, founder of *Chabad*, thus taught that the commandment "You shall love your fellow like yourself" (Leviticus 19:18) is a means and prerequisite to the commandment "You shall love G-d, your G-d" (Deuteronomy 6:5).[13] The act of material and spiritual *tzedakah* (charity) effects that "*Tzedakah* exalts a people" (Proverbs 14:34);[14] that is, the benefactor's mind and heart will be purified ('exalted') a thousandfold.[15]

---

12. *Ibid.*, p. 105 (Vayechi, sect. VII).
13. *Hayom Yom*, p. 93. *Likutei Sichot* II:p. 298. See also *Keter Shem Tov*, Hossafot, par. 18.
14. R. Shneur Zalman of Liadi, *Torah Or*, Bereishit, p. 1b*f*. Cf. *Tanchuma* on Exodus 22:24.
15. *Likutei Sichot* I:p. 262 (Kedoshim, sect. XIX).

II

Spiritual Charity

The concept of 'spiritual charity' is a constantly recurring theme. In one of his first pastoral letters[16] the Rebbe writes:

> Man possesses a body and soul. Just as there is material poverty (in food, clothing, shelter), so there is spiritual poverty where the deficiency is in spiritual things: knowledge of Torah, observance of *mitzvot*, and the practice of good deeds.

The Rebbe then refers to the Midrashic interpretation of Isaiah's statement of the ordinances of righteousness that bring man close to G-d — "Is it not to deal your bread to the

---

16. Dated 18 Elul 5710; reprinted in *Outlines of the Social and Communal Work of Chabad Lubavitch* (Kehot: New York 1953), p. 48. Cf. *Likutei Sichot* IV:p. 1059.

hungry and that you bring the cast-out poor to your house! When you see the naked that you cover him, and that you hide not yourself from your own flesh"(Isaiah 58:7):

> *The hungry refers to him that is famished of Torah, and bread refers to the Torah.. If there be a person that understands Torah he is to provide others, too, from his Torah.. How are we to understand 'When you see the naked..'? Surely in the sense of when you see a man lacking in the knowledge of Torah, take him into your house and teach him to say the* Shema *and prayers, and teach him daily one verse or one law, and encourage him to fulfill the* mitzvot. *For none is naked in Israel but he who lacks Torah and* mitzvot.[17]

The constant emphasis on 'spiritual charity' is not to belittle in any way the plain sense of the *mitzvah* to render material assistance: One of the ways to befriend and bring another closer to Torah is by extending a helping hand to offer physical and material succor. This is not only an essential part of the obligation of *ahavat Yisrael* but also helps to bring him closer to spiritual truth. Nonetheless, one is not to wait and make material aid dependent on spiritual consequences. We must help others materially without any preconditions.[18]

---

17. *Eliyahu Rabba*, ch. 27. Cf. ibid., ch. 13; *Pirkei deR. Eliezer*, ch. 19; *Bi'ur Hagra* on *Shulchan Aruch*, Yoreh De'ah 245:3. See also *Zohar* II:129a (and *Nitzutzei Orot, ad loc.*) that to tend to the spiritual welfare of those in need thereof excels the provision of material needs; and R. Dov Ber of Mezhirech, *Or Torah*, sect. 486.

18. *Likutei Sichot* I:p. 262 (Kedoshim, sect. XVIII). *Cf.* also *ibid.*, p. 133f (Bo, sect. XIII-XVII).

III

Divine Providence

The Baal Shem Tov taught that the *mitzvah* of *ahavat Yisrael* applies even to our relationship with a Jew at the furthest end of the world whom one has never seen.[19] R. Dov Ber, the Maggid of Mezhirech, taught that this means to love even a totally wicked person like a completely righteous one.[20] All this is especially incumbent upon those led by Divine Providence to places where Torah and *mitzvot* are weak and negligible. A person like that may possibly argue that he needs to protect himself and seek to escape from such places, saying "I will save my own soul." Thus he must realize that he is dealing with a matter of *pikuach*

---

19. *Keter Shem Tov*, Hossafot, par. 140. *Likutei Sichot* I:p. 201 (Vayechi, sect. X); and II:pp. 435 and 686.
20. *Or Torah*, Hossafot, par. 42. *Cf.* R. Mosheh Cordovero, *Tomer Devorah*, ch. 2; and "The Dynamics of *Ahavat Yisrael*," sect. XI. See *Likutei Sichot* II:p. 299.

nefashot, of saving lives.[21] In cases of *pikuach nefashot* one is not permitted to make such calculations.[22]

The fact that Divine Providence has led him to that place implies that Providence has charged him with a mission, and also endowed him with the abilities to convert that place to one of Torah and *mitzvot*. To teach us this truism, the Talmud[23] relates how Rav came to Babylon and "found there an open field," i.e., places where the people were ignorant and negligent in the observance of the laws of Sabbath, dietary laws, and so forth — "and he put a fence around it," i.e., he instituted enactments to prevent them from further transgressions.[24]

The Talmud[25] relates also of R. Chanina bar Pappa that he wished to experience the spiritual achievements of R. Joshua ben Levi. R. Chanina had observed everything that is written in the Torah, and, indeed, when his soul passed to its eternal rest a pillar of fire formed a partition between him and the world.[26] Nonetheless, he did not attain his wish. For R. Chanina could not answer affirmatively the question, "Have you attached yourself to the sufferers of *ra'atan* (a contagious disease with repugnant symptoms) and engaged thus in Torah?" Many sages, the Talmud informs us, had distanced themselves from people afflicted with that disease.

---

21. *Cf.* Midrashim on Numbers 25:17; *Sifre*, Tetze, par. 252. See also *Zohar* II:139a, and the next note.
22. See *Yoma* 82a. *Cf. Sanhedrin* 73a and 74a.
23. *Eruvin* 6a and 100b; and *Chulin* 110a. See Rashi *ad loc.*
24. *Likutei Sichot* I:p. 262 (Kedoshim, sect. XIX). See below, note 32.
25. *Ketuvot* 77b.
26. The *Gemara, ad loc.*, explains that this happens only to the one, or at most two, most outstanding men in a generation.

R. Joshua ben Levi, however, attached himself to these sufferers and studied the Torah. He sought to disseminate Torah everywhere, even among those suffering from *ra'atan*, and that is why he merited what he did.

That, too, is reflected in the instruction of R. Joshua ben Levi, in *Perek Kinyan Hatorah*,[27] that one must be *preoccupied with Torah*, i.e., not just learn for oneself but to disseminate Torah even unto the very lowest level of the 'sufferers of *ra'atan*.'[28]

However, this principle is by no means to be understood in terms that one is to neglect oneself and go out of his way to be preoccupied with others only. For one thing, the above-cited prooftext of Isaiah 58 ends with the exhortation "Hide not yourself from your own flesh." This means that one may not ignore, and must work on, one's own 'fleshness,' one's own involvement with the mundane.[29] Moreover, one must never force oneself — *of oneself* — into 'narrow straits.' To be sure, there is always a lot to be achieved. At the same time, however, "all roads are presumed to be dangerous,"[30] thus why expose yourself intentionally to danger!

If, however, it be that "he went down into Egypt compelled *by decree*,"[31] i.e., that he was told and sent there, or he finds that Divine Providence has led him to that particular place, then all these arguments fall by the side.

---

27. *Avot* 6:2.
28. *Likutei Sichot* IV:p. 1239.
29. *Ibid.*, p. 1059.
30. *Yerushalmi, Berachot* 4:4.
31. *Haggadah.* See Genesis 46:3, and commentaries *ad loc.; Zohar* II:53a.

After all, it is "by Divine decree."³² He must realize that coming there 'by decree' he is under compulsion, going only because of the decree. Hence he must do so joyfully. He is assured that "I will also surely bring you up again" (Genesis 46:4), and in the end he will come out "with great substance" (Genesis 15:14) spiritually as well as materially.³³

---

32. This follows the fundamental Chassidic doctrine of *hashgachah peratit*, Divine Providence embracing every particular thing. The Baal Shem Tov interpreted the verse "A man's goings are established by G-d.." (Psalms 37:23) to mean that wherever man happens to be, regardless of any personal reasons that prompted him to go there, it is really Divine Providence that brought him to that particular place in order to serve some spiritual purpose. See *Me'or Einayim*, Vayakhel (*Sefer Baal Shem Tov*, Lech Lecha, par. 20*ff.*); *Keter Shem Tov*, Hossafot, par. 3; *Hayom Yom*, p. 104. See also *Keter Shem Tov*, par. 46 and 220, and *ibid.*, Hossafot, par. 119-129. *Cf.* the Rebbe's detailed analysis of the concept of *hashgachah peratit* in *Likutei Sichot*, VIII:pp. 277-284.
33. *Likutei Sichot* IV:p. 1220.

IV

What Is A Chassid?

The previous Lubavitcher Rebbe, R. Joseph Isaac, who brought Chabad-Lubavitch to America, once recalled[34] a thought-provoking conversation between his father and predecessor, R. Sholom Dov-Ber, and a Chassid:

> The Chassid asked: "Rebbe, what is a Chassid?"
>
> R. Sholom Dov-Ber answered: "A Chassid is a street-lamp-lighter. A street-lamp-lighter has a pole with fire. He knows that the fire is not his own, and he goes around lighting all lamps on his route."
>
> The Chassid asked: "But what if the lamp is in a desolate wilderness?"
>
> The Rebbe answered: "Then, too, one must light it.

---

34. *Sefer Hasichot 5701*, p. 136f.

Let it be noted that there is a wilderness, and let the wilderness feel ashamed before the light."

"But what if the lamp is in the midst of a sea?"

"Then one must take off the clothes, jump into the water and light it there!"

"And that is a Chassid?"

The Rebbe thought for a long moment and then said: "Yes, that is a Chassid."

The Chassid continued: "Rebbe, I see no lamps!"

"That is because you are not a street-lamp-lighter."

"How does one become such?"

The Rebbe replied: "One must be sur mera *(avoid evil). When beginning with oneself, cleansing oneself, becoming more refined, then one sees the lamp of the other. When, Heaven forbid, one is crude, then one sees but crudeness; but when himself noble, one sees nobility."*[35]

When the present Rebbe recounted this conversation, he added: The lamps are there, but they need to be lit. It is written, "The soul of man is a lamp of G-d" (Proverbs 20:27), and it is also written, "A *mitzvah* is a lamp and the

---

35. This again reflects typical Chassidic thought. The Baal Shem Tov (in comment on *Avot* 4:1; *Nega'im* 2:5; and *Kidushin* 70a) teaches that what man sees in another is a mirror-reflection of himself: as he is himself, so he sees the other. Divine Providence brought him to see it in order to correct his own deficiencies. See *Keter Shem Tov*, par. 89, 116, 302, and 363; *Sefer Baal Shem Tov*, Bereishit, par. 123*ff.*

Torah is light" (Proverbs 6:23). A Chassid is he who puts his personal affairs aside and goes around lighting up the souls of Jews with the light of Torah and *mitzvot*. Jewish souls are in readiness to be lit. Sometimes they are around the corner. Sometimes they are in a wilderness or at sea. But there must be someone who disregards personal comforts and conveniences and goes out to put a light to these lamps. That is the function of a true Chassid.[36]

Chassidism in general demands that one disseminate Torah and *Yiddishkeit* all over and seek to benefit fellow-Jews. In the words of R. Sholom Dov-Ber: "A Chassid is he who surrenders his self to seeking the welfare of another."[37] Over and beyond that, *Chabad* demands *pnimiyut* (inwardness): one should not act superficially, as a mere act of faith, but with inner conviction, with the soul-faculties of *chabad*.[38] One must involve even the rational faculties of the animal soul, and even the physical brain of the body. This is the mystical concept of 'the Divine soul entering the physical body.'[39]

---

36. *Sichot* of 13 Tamuz 5722 (printed in *Or Hachassidut*, Kehot: Kfar Chabad 1965, p. 215*ff*.). *Cf. Likutei Sichot* II:p. 315*f*.
37. *Sefer Hasichot* 5700, p. 33. This reflects R. Shneur Zalman of Liadi's definition of a *Chassid* in terms of the Talmudic statement (*Nidah* 17a) that he who burns his nails is a *chassid*, as explained there by *Tossafot; Likutei Diburim*, vol. I, p. 135. See *Likutei Sichot* XI:pp. 85 and 87.
38. *Chochmah* (conceptual wisdom), *Binah* (comprehensive understanding), *Da'at* (penetrating knowledge and conscious awareness of the *chochmah* expanded by *binah*, to the point of bringing it to its logical conclusion in actual implementation) — *Tanya*, ch. 3; see *Mystical Concepts in Chassidism*, ch. III: sect. 4. These are the foundation underlying the philosophical and psychological system of Lubavitch Chassidism, which, therefore, is referred to as *Chabad*-Chassidism.
39. *Likutei Sichot* III:p. 800*f. Cf.* also the saying of R. Dov Ber of

V

Offensive *vs.* Defensive

At this point we have a clear definition of what it means to be a Chassid and what the Chassid's task and mission in life is. But how is he to set out to realize his ideal? The answer to this question is found in the following quotations from the Rebbe:

> The essential features of the attitude and policy of Lubavitch are not to content ourselves with defensive tactics. That is to say, not to wait until a position of *Yiddishkeit* is attacked in order to rally to its defense. This has been the erroneous attitude of American orthodox Jewry and also of Jewries in certain Euro-

---

Lubavitch: "*Chabad* means intellectualization, comprehensive understanding and a profound, absorbing delving into. Exert yourself, and you will be a Chassid!" *Hatamim* V:p. 102 (526).

> pean countries. The proper attitude is to employ offensive and preventative methods through the widest possible dissemination of, and propagation for, those high ideals for which the classical Torah-tradition stands. As a logical corollary of this attitude it follows that we cannot remain content with activity confined to our own, immediate circle. Propagation of Torah-Judaism must be directed at all strata of Jewry.[40]

In a conversation in the summer of 1951, the Rebbe dealt with this same point at greater length:

Orthodox Jewry has unfortunately concentrated upon defensive strategy. We were always worried lest we lose positions and strongholds. And indeed we had all reason for worry. One Jewish bastion after another had fallen into the hands of the non-religious. Had orthodox Jews, instead of waiting to defend, taken the initiative and sought to widen their influence and created more and better bastions for Torah-*Yiddishkeit*, the situation would be quite different and the non-religious would not, as is now the case, dominate Jewish communal affairs.

> The lesson to be drawn from this is obvious. To discharge ourselves of our duty we must take the initiative. This, of course, takes courage, planning, vision and the will to carry on despite all odds.

> But that has always been the true Jewish approach, the Torah perspective on life and the ways of Divine

---

40. Quoted in C. Raddock, "Bridging the Gap between East and West," *The Jewish Forum*, December 1953.

Providence. If we were to count the odds and weigh the chances, we would be lacking in *bitachon* — faith in the ultimate affirmation of the right and justification of the just.

Weakness, lack of power and influence, should never deter us from the path prescribed by the Torah. We must not be frightened by the fact that only a minority of the millions of Jews gathered in this country are to be counted as Torah-conscious Jews. We must know only one thing: our task and our will to do it. Success is not up to us; it is in higher hands.

The thing we have to fear most at this moment is the defeatism and the defection that has gripped some of our best elements in this country in the face of the growing effects of so-called 'inter-faith' movements, and the watering down of the very content of our religion to a point where our children will no longer know whether they are Jews or not. This defeatism is even worse than the limitations to defensive tactics.

Charity begins at home. We cannot talk of assuming responsibility for the rest of the Jewish world, of building new centers for Torah and *Yiddishkeit* elsewhere, even in *Eretz Yisrael*, if right here in our midst our brothers and sisters are being engulfed. More than that, we have no right to teach and lead others if at home we neglect the very thing we want to make others do.[41]

The offensive for Torah-Judaism that the Rebbe speaks

---

41. Quoted in G. Kranzler, "A Visit with the new Lubavitcher Rebbe," *Jewish Life*, Sept.-Oct. 1951.

of is directed at all Jews, regardless of their background and present status. For one thing, all Jews in unison are one body, the individual members of which interact and are most intimately related to one another. The acts and affectations of any one of them affect directly every other one as well.[42]

Also, there is not a single Jew, as far as he may seem or consider himself to have drifted from the center of *Yiddishkeit*, who does not have some good point, some particular *mitzvah* which by nature or inclination he may promote. This spark of 'good' in each soul can and must be utilized for the good of the Jewish community, and, in turn, for the good of the person who does it.[43] Each individual counts, because each individual may perhaps become a leader or the father of many generations to be gained for the Torah, or Heaven forbid — to be lost.[44]

The Rebbe sees the non-orthodox not only as the objects but also as subjects of the call to arms for Torah-*Yiddishkeit*.

> For example, take the danger of mixed marriages. If we can use even those of our people who do not believe in any other of the 613 *mitzvot* than the preservation of the purity of our families, we must definitely call on them in order to be able to stem

---

42. *Likutei Sichot* II:pp. 297-301, 398ff. and 435. See *Mechilta deRashby* on Exodus 19:6: "They are as one body and one soul.. if one of them is afflicted all of them feel it.." See also *Vayikra Rabba* 4:6, and *Zohar* III:122a. Cf. R. Menachem Mendel of Lubavitch (Tzemach Tzedek), *Derech Mitzvotecha*, s.v. Ahavat Yisrael.
43. See note 41.
44. Ibid. Cf. *Sanhedrin* 37a.

such defections from our faith and with it from our nation. Not always does it matter who does the 'doing,' as long as it is done. The accomplishment counts for what it achieves objectively and for what it does to the one involved. (The same would apply to Jewish education — that whoever has the power and the will to contribute some aspect, some particular skill or capacity towards the offensive for Jewish education, must be drawn upon.)[45]

---

45. *Ibid.*

VI
"Words From The Heart Enter The Heart"

The obvious questions that rise now are: how does one approach non-religious Jews to become involved and more observant? Even while allowing for individual gains to be made, what realistic hopes are there for the success of such an offensive for Torah-*Yiddishkeit*? At times it would seem that for every one won over, the Chassid probably meets up with perhaps two disappointments as well. How, then, does one retain the courage and enthusiasm to carry on if the odds are so heavily weighted against?

The Rebbe states that it is a well-known empirical fact that where matters of Torah and *mitzvot* are concerned every Jew, no matter how estranged, is generally found responsive.[46] To be sure, one Jew may more readily respond to one

---

46. See Maimonides, *Hilchot Gerushin* 2:20, where this maxim is

particular *mitzvah* or idea, while a second one will respond to another. It is all a matter of experience and approach. But where the approach is right, no Jew is wholly unresponsive! For no Jew is absolutely stripped of every vestige of Jewishness.[47]

It would serve no purpose to approach the non-observant with demands for immediate, full ascent to a perfect Torah-way of life. But through a pleasant, understanding and helpful approach, a good many of these straying souls can be brought back partially, and gradually even completely. However, this is possible only if we take the initiative and if we do not fall into the trap of overlooking the trees because of the forest.[48]

The most important thing is "no compromise"! Compromise is dangerous because it sickens both the body and the soul. A compromiser who tries to mediate religion and environment is unable to go in either direction and unable to distinguish the truth.[49] A fault yet more serious is to sanctify the compromise, to still the conscience, and to leave no possibility for *teshuvah* (return).[50] The Rebbe states that

> It is important to know that one must do everything, but at the same time we welcome the doing of even a

---

stated in Halachic context. Hence the oft-cited principle in *Chabad*-Chassidism that "it is innate to every Jew that he does not want — nor is he able — to separate himself from Divinity;" see *Maamar Bati Legani 5713*, ch. 2, 4 and 5f.

47. Raddock, *op. cit.*
48. Kranzler, *op. cit.*
49. Quoted in H. Weiner, "The Lubavitcher Movement —II," *Commentary*, April 1957, p. 327.
50. *Ibid.*, p. 318.

part. If all we can accomplish is to save one limb, we save that. Then we worry about saving another.[51]

This strict adherence and allegiance to the principles and precepts of the Torah in the perspective of the historical tradition of orthodoxy, by no means implies that orthodoxy in general, and Chassidism in particular, are to be seen as 'fossilized conservatism':

> I do not believe that other movements are liberal and that orthodox means conservative. The meaning of 'conservatism' is someone who is so petrified he cannot accept something new. But true Judaism, Halachah or Torah, encompasses all the universe, and it encompasses every new invention, every new theory, every new piece of knowledge or thought or action. Everything that happens in 1972 has a place in the Torah, and it must be interpreted, it must be explained, it must be evaluated from the point of view of Torah, even if it happened for the first time in March 1972.[52]

The distant future, or special measures to guarantee success, and even temporary setbacks, do not seem to be the immediate concern of the Chassidim. As the Rebbe puts it:

> *We can see only what is going on right now, in the present, and on the surface. The patterns of Divine Providence are not unveiled to us till later. Our task, and in particular that of Jewish youth, is to do and to want to do. The rest is not up to us. But, to cite the*

---

51. *Ibid.*, p. 327.
52. Quoted in *New York Times*, March 27, 1972, p. 39.

The Philosophy of Lubavitch Activism

late Lubavitcher Rebbe (R. Joseph Isaac), of sainted memory, we have two basic assurances. The first is that one action is worth more than a thousand sighs. And secondly, no action for a good purpose has ever been done in vain. In the long run it will succeed and pay its dividends. These must be our guiding principles.[53]

We ourselves do not count. It is our task, our sacred mission, that matters. And if we but want to carry it on, our goal will not remain unachieved.[54]

If all the *mitzvot* of the Torah must be carried out with vigor, then *a fortiori* the *mitzvah* of *ahavat Yisrael*, the very foundation of the Torah.[55] One must speak with fellow-Jews about Torah and *mitzvot*, and, if unsuccessful, speak again. Even if someone should react antagonistically, do not be discouraged. On the contrary: his antagonism only proves that he is affected.[56] Thus one must speak to him again and again until he accedes.[57]

---

53. Kranzler, *op. cit.* For these aphorisms of R. Joseph Isaac, see *Hayom Yom*, pp. 31, 35, and 95.
54. *Ibid.*
55. See *Shabbat* 31a; *Sifra* on Leviticus 19:18; *Tanya*, ch. 32. See "The Dynamics of *Ahavat Yisrael*," sect. XIII-XIV.
56. For as long as some reaction is evoked, this is an indication that the person is affected and impressible. It is difficult to reach the indifferent, impassable person. See R. Sholom Dov-Ber, *Torat Shalom*, p. 10f.
57. "Whence do we know that if one sees something unseemly in another one is obliged to reprove him? Because it is said, 'You shall surely rebuke..' (Levit. 19:17). If he rebuked him but he did not accept it, whence do we know that he must rebuke him again? The text states '*hoche'ach tochi'ach* — rebuke, you shall rebuke' — anyhow," (*Arachin* 16b) even a hundred times (*Baba*

One must go about this vigorously. To be sure, in order to be heard and acceptable one must speak gently and in a pleasant manner, but also with conviction and vigor. With this combination of pleasantness and vigor one will succeed.

> When not successful at first, one must realize that the fault lies not with the other but within yourself. The other is receptive, but because your own words "do not come from the heart" that is why "they do not enter the heart."[58]

In the perspective of this goal and sense of responsibility, odds just do not count and may not count.

Metzia 31a). One is not permitted, though .. to do so harshly and to put him to shame, as the Scriptural verse concludes "do not suffer sin because of him;" (*Arachin* 16b; *Sifra* on this verse; *Tanchuma*, Mishpatim:7). See *Zohar* III:86a, and Maimonides, *Hilchot De'ot* 6:8. See also *Keter Shem Tov*, sect. 113, 131, 251, 262 and 389; *Or Torah*, sect. 117 and 486. Cf. "The Dynamics of *Ahavat Yisrael*," note 26 and sect. III.

58. *Likutei Sichot* I:p. 128f. (Bo, sect. III).

VII

The Rebbe: A Soul-Geologist

What is the role of a *Rebbe* in this context? If such comparison be permissible, it would seem to be that of a "chief street-lamp-lighter."

Every Jew has the "soul of man that is a lamp of G-d," though there are some among them that wait until it be lit for them. That is the function of the *nesi'ey Yisrael* (the leaders of Israel; the *Rebbes*): to light the Divine lamp in every Jew. Just as in the *menorah* there are seven different branches, so, too, there are seven different groups of Jews,[59] each with its own peculiar traits, needs and approach. The *Rebbe's* role is to light them all.[60]

---

59. For this homily see at length R. Shneur Zalman of Liadi, *Likutei Torah*, Beha'alotecha, p. 32d. Cf. *Sefer Baal Shem Tov*, Behar, note 1.
60. *Likutei Sichot* II:p. 315 f. Cf. *Tanchuma*, ed. Buber, Pinchas: 1; *Tanchuma*, Pincas: 11; *Bamidbar Rabba* 21:15.

In a similar, though differently worded way, the Rebbe once answered a group of students that had asked him this very question:

> The Jewish people are referred as *eretz cheifetz* (a land of delight; or a land of treasure; Malachi 3:12). In the earth lie concealed many treasures, but they are not visible on the surface and one must dig deeply in order to find them. However, not everyone knows the right places where to dig for them. Some explore and in the end find only swampy waters and mire, as happened, for example, to Dr. Freud when he delved into the labyrinth of man's psyche. Others again wind up with nothing but rocks, as happened, for example, to Dr. Adler who found but a striving for superiority directed toward strength and dominance. Only an expert knows where to dig so as to find the truly precious treasures: silver — signifying love of G-d; gold — signifying reverence of G-d; and diamonds — which allude to the essence-faith. To find these treasures, that is the task of a *Rebbe*.[61]

The role of a *Rebbe*, then, is that of a soul-geologist who manifests the latent powers and treasures concealed in all, who seeks to awaken in everyone the potential he has. He is the generator that charges and a beacon that guides, in whom all the above is succinctly crystallized. His role as mentor and counselor, whose advice and blessing is sought in matters spiritual and material, is seen in the same context: the context of responsibility toward his people.

---

61. *MS*, and *Ma'ariv*, 16 January 1970, p. 29. Note also the Baal Shem Tov's interpretation of this verse, in *Keter Shem Tov*, Hossafot, par. 44.

The Philosophy of Lubavitch Activism 211

When asked how he can possibly reply to the multifarious concerns ranging from questions of theology and metaphysics to family- and business-affairs, the Rebbe replied that, for one thing, he is not afraid to answer "I do not know." But above all —

> If I do know, then I have no right not to answer. When someone comes to you for help and you can help him to the best of your knowledge, and you refuse him this help, then you also become a cause of his suffering.[62]

But even while the *Rebbe's* role is central, at no times should his presence give rise to some form of personality-cult. Chassidim are not to rely for themselves on the *Rebbe's* efforts. *Chabad*-Chassidism in particular demands that a Jew attain all positive qualities by means of personal effort.[63] One must not be content even with natural good-

---

62. *New York Times*, ad loc.
63. This, too, reflects classic Chassidic thought, i.e., the original teachings of the Baal Shem Tov and the Maggid of Mezhirech: they refer to the Patriarchs as models from whom we are to learn *not* to rely on faith and tradition alone. Thus we refer in the *Amidah* to "G-d of Abraham, G-d of Isaac, and G-d of Jacob," and do not compound all three together. This is to teach us that Isaac did not rely on the tradition of Abraham alone, nor did Jacob simply rely on the heritage from his predecessors. Each exerted himself to understand his heritage so as to arrive at his own knowledge and beliefs through personal labour and efforts. Thus Isaac did not simply follow the "G-d of Abraham" but made Him his own, "G-d of Isaac," and likewise with Jacob. See *Keter Shem Tov*, sect. 206; and *Or Torah*, sect. 255. Cf. R. Isaiah Horowitz, *Shenei Luchot Haberit*, Be'Assarah Maamarot, ch. 1, on I-Chronicles 28:9 (p. 29c). See also "The Concept of the *Rebbe-Tzadik* in Chassidism," sect. IX.

ness, i.e., with that which comes to man naturally and easily. Everyone must exert himself in the service of G-d, both physically as well as spiritually, as it is written, "Man is born to toil" (Job 5:7).[64]

The objective of every individual must be to act and to actualize. Moreover, one should not simply act, but do so with the effort which the Torah refers to as *amal* (toil). Only then does man raise himself from the level of *adam* (man) — "dust from the *adamah* (ground; earth)" (Genesis 2:7) to the level of *adam* — "*edameh* (I shall be like) the Most High)" (Isaiah 14:14),[65] as it were.[66] As the Rebbe proclaimed the day he assumed leadership:

> Chabad has always demanded that everyone must act himself, and not to depend on the *Rebbes*.[67]

---

64. *Likutei Sichot* III:p. 800f. Cf. ibid., II:p. 485.
65. An etymological interpretation of *adam*, frequent in mystical literature. See *Shenei Luchot Haberit*, Toldot Adam (ed. Jerusalem 1963, vol. I:p. 3b): "When man attaches himself to Above and likens himself unto Him, blessed be He, by walking in His paths (see Deuteronomy 13:5, and *Shabbat* 133b), he is then called by the essential name *adam* which is an idiom of *edameh le'Elyon* (Isaiah 14:14) .. But if he separates himself from the attachment, he is then called *adam* in relation to *adamah* (ground; soil) from which he was taken (see *Bereishit Rabba* 17:4) — dust he is and unto dust he shall return. The principal purpose, however, is for the term *adam* to indicate *edameh le'Elyon*." See also *ibid.*, Tzon Yossef (vol. II:p. 29a): "The name *adam* originally indicated *edameh le'Elyon*; but after Adam sinned, it indicates the earthly character of 'dust from the ground.'" Cf. *Zohar* III:48a (and *Nitzutzei Zohar*, ad loc.), that *adam* is the highest designation of man; and see R. Shmuel of Lubavitch, *Torat Shmuel-5629*, p. 155. Cf. also *Hayom Yom*, p. 84.
66. Pastoral Letter of 11 Nissan 5732.
67. This fundamental principle of *Chabad*-Chassidism, demanding

Thus all of us need to act personally, with the 248 limbs and 365 veins of the body and the 248 'limbs' and 365 'veins' of the soul.. *Each one* must convert the folly of the 'opposing side' and the vehemence of the animal soul to holiness.

Moses could have built the sanctuary all by himself, but he wished for all Jews to have the merit of participating.. Thus it is self-evident that in fulfilling our duty to establish an Abode for Divinity here on earth, all of us, and *all Jews*, must partake. Everyone must act himself and carry out his mission.[68]

In a paraphrase of the maxim that "everything depends on the will,"[69] the Rebbe states:

It is not we who count — we with our weaknesses and limited capacities. It is our will to do a task that we realize is important. Success is not in our hands, it

---

personal effort and achievement as opposed to reliance on the *Rebbe-Tzadik*, is one of the major differences between *Chabad-*Chassidism and the Chassidic schools classified as *Chagat* — (acronym for *Chessed-Gevurah-Tiferet* — the basic emotive traits) Chassidism (colloquially often referred to as 'Polish Chassidism'). The latter adopted the principle of "'The *tzadik* — *yichyeh* by his faith' (Habakuk 2:4) — do not read *yichyeh* (lives), but *yechayeh* (animates; bestows life and vitality)." See *Likutei Diburim*, vol. I:p. 282. See also the extensive correspondence between R. Shneur Zalman of Liadi and R. Levi Yitzchak of Berdichev on the one hand, and R. Abraham of Kalisk on the other, in *Igarot Ba'al Hatanya Ubnei Doro*, ed. D. Hilman, Jerusalem 1953, nos. 58-59, 100, and 102-103.

68. *Likutei Sichot* II:p. 500f.
69. Zohar II:162b. *Cf. Megilah* 6b; Maimonides, *Hilchot Teshuvah* 5:1.

is G-d's. But we have to will to do what He demands of us, and in that will all our weaknesses and insufficiencies wane and become insignificant.[70]

---

70. Kranzler, *ibid*. This statement may be taken as a succinct synopsis of the Rebbe's approach and attitude, reflecting his ever-recurring theme that *"hama'aseh hu ha'ikkar* — action, actual doing, is the essential thing!" (*Avot* 1:17; see *Zohar* I:99b).

BIBLIOGRAPHY and INDEXES

BIBLIOGRAPHY

AVODAT HAKODESH, R. Meir ibn Gabbai, Jerusalem 1954
BEN PORAT YOSEF, R. Yaakov Yosef of Polnoy, New York 1954
BESHA'AH SHEHIKDIMU-5672, R. Sholom Dov Ber of Lubavitch, Brooklyn NY 1977
BET ELOKIM, R. Mosheh of Torani (*Mabit*), Warsaw 1831
BIUREI HAZOHAR-TZEMACH TZEDEK, R. Menachem Mendel of Lubavitch, Brooklyn NY 1968-78
BUTZINA DINEHURA, Anthology of teachings of R. Baruch of Medzyboz, Levov 1880
CHAZON ISH, R. Abraham Isaiah Karelitz, Bnei Berak 1980
CHIDUSHEI AGADOT, R. Judah Loewe (*Maharal*), London 1960
CHOMAT ANOCH, R. Chaim Yosef David Azulay (*Chida*), Jerusalem 1965
DARKEI TZEDEK, R. Zechariah Mendel of Yeraslov, Warsaw 1877
DA'AT MOSHEH, R. Mosheh Elyakim of Kozinetz, Levov 1879
DEGEL MACHANEH EPHRAYIM, R. Mosheh Chaim Ephraim of Sudylkov, Jerusalem 1963
DERECH CHAYIM, R. Dov Ber of Lubavitch, Brooklyn NY 1955
DERECH MITZVOTECHAH, R. Menachem Mendel (*Tzemach Tzedek*) of Lubavitch, Brooklyn NY 1953
DIBRAT SHELOMOH, R. Shelomoh of Lutzk, Zolkiev 1848
DUDA'IM BASADEH, R. Reuben Horowitz of Dzyarnovic, Levov 1859
EINAYIM LAMISHPAT, R. Yitzchak Arieli, Jerusalem 1963 *e.s.*
EMUNOT VEDE'OT, R. Saadiah Gaon, Josefow 1885
EVEN SHELEMAH, Anthology of teachings of R. Elijah of Vilna, Jerusalem 1960
HAYOM YOM, R. Menachem M. Schneerson *shalita* of Lubavitch, Brooklyn NY 1961
IGAROT BAAL HATANYA UBNEI DORO, ed. D. Z. Hilman, Jerusalem 1953

IGERET HAKODESH, part IV of *Tanya, s.v.*
IGERET HATESHUVAH, part III of *Tanya, s.v.*
IGROT KODESH ADMUR HATZEMACH TZEDEK, R. Menachem Mendel of Lubavitch, Brooklyn NY 1980
IGROT KODESH ADMUR HAZAKEN, R. Shneur Zalman of Liadi, Brooklyn NY 1980
IKKARIM, R. Joseph Albo, Vilna n.d.
KEDUSHAT LEVI, R. Levi Yitzchak of Berdichev, Jerusalem 1964
KETER SHEM TOV, Anthology of Teachings of R. Israel Baal Shem Tov, Brooklyn NY 1987
KITZURIM VEHE'AROT LESEFER TANYA, R. Menachem Mendel of Lubavitch, Brooklyn NY 1948
KOVETZ TESHUVOT HARAMBAM, R. Mosheh Maimonides, Leipzig 1859
KUZARY, R. Judah Halevi, Tel Aviv 1959
LIKUTEI AMARIM, see MAGGID DEVARAV LEYA'AKOV
LIKUTEI DIBURIM, R. Yosef Yitzchak of Lubavitch, Brooklyn NY 1957
LIKUTEI SHOSHANAH, see NO'AM ELIMELECH
LIKUTEI SICHOT, R. Menachem M. Schneerson *shalita* of Lubavitch, Brooklyn NY 1962 *e.s.*
LIKUTEI TORAH, R. Shneur Zalman of Liadi, Brooklyn NY 1965
LIKUTEI TORAH VETA'AMEI HAMITZVOT, R. Chaim Vital, Tel Aviv 1963
LIKUTIM YEKARIM, Anthology of Teachings of R. Israel Baal Shem Tov, the Maggid, and others, ed. Toldot Aharon, Jerusalem 1974
MAGEN AVOT, R. Shimon Duran, Livorno 1763
MAGGID DEVARAV LEYA'AKOV, Anthology of Teachings of R. Dov Ber, the Maggid of Mezhirech, ed. Kehot, Brooklyn NY 1979
MAYIM RABIM-5636, R. Shmuel of Lubavitch, Brooklyn NY 1946
MEGALEH AMUKOT, R. Nathan Schapiro, Lublin 1912
MENORAT HAMA'OR R. Israel ibn Al-Nakawa, New York 1929-32
MIDBAR KEDEMOT, R. Chaim Yosef David Azulay (*Chida*), Jerusalem 1962
MIDRASH SECHEL TOV, R. Menachem ben Shelomoh, New York 1959
MINCHAT CHINUCH, R. Yosef Babad, New York 1962
MINEI TARGUMA, R. Isaiah Berlin, Vilna 1836
MITZVOT HASHEM, R. Jonathan Steif, Pietrokov 1931
MOREH NEVUCHIM, R. Mosheh Maimonides, Jerusalem 1960
NETIVOT OLAM, R. Judah Loew (*Maharal*), London 1961
NO'AM ELIMELECH, R. Elimelech of Lizhensk, Jerusalem 1960
NO'AM MAGADIM, R. Eleazar Horowitz of Tarnograd, Levov 1807
OR HACHAMAH, R. Abraham Azulay, Przemysl 1896
OR HASHEM, R. Chasdai Crescas, Tel Aviv 1963
OR HATORAH, R. Menachem Mendel of Lubavitch, Brooklyn NY 1960 *e.s..*

BIBLIOGRAPHY

OR HA'EMET, Anthology of Teachings of the Maggid of Mezhirech, New York 1960

OR TORAH, Anthology of Teachings of the Maggid of Mezhirech, ed. Kehot, Brooklyn NY 1979

OTZAR HAGE'ONIM-CHAGIGAH, ed. B. Lewin, Jerusalem 1932

PACHAD YITZCHAK, R. Yitzchak Lampronti, ed. Venice, Jerusalem n.d.

PARDES RIMONIM, R. Mosheh Cordovero, Jerusalem 1962

PERI EITZ CHAYIM, R. Chaim Vital, ed. Koritz: Jerusalem 1960, and ed. Jerusalem 1980

PRI HA'ARETZ, R. Menachem Mendel of Vitebsk, Levov 1864

RAMBAN AL HATORAH, R. Mosheh Nachmanides, Jerusalem 1959

R. BACHAYA AL HATORAH, R. Bachya ben Asher, Jerusalem 1959

REISHIT CHOCHMAH, R. Elijah de Vidas, Amsterdam 1708

RESHIMOT AL SHIR HASHIRIM, R. Menachem Mendel of Lubavitch, Brooklyn NY 1960

ROKE'ACH HAGADOL, R. Eleazar of Worms, Warsaw 1880

ROSH AMANAH, R. Yitzchak Abarbanel, Tel Aviv 1958

SDEI CHEMED, R. Chaim Chizkiyahu Medini, Brooklyn NY 1959

SEDER HADOROT HECHADASH, M. Bodak, ? 1941

SEFER BAAL SHEM TOV, Anthology of Teachings of R. Israel Baal Shem Tov, Landsberg 1948

SEFER CHAREIDIM, R. Eleazar Azkari, Jerusalem 1958

SEFER CHASSIDIM, R. Yehudah Hachassid. ed. Margolius, Jerusalem 1957

SEFER HACHAKIRAH, R. Menachem Mendel of Lubavitch, Brooklyn NY 1955

SEFER HACHINUCH, R. Aharon Halevi of Barcelona, New York 1962

SEFER HALIKUTIM, Anthology of teachings of R. Menachem Mendel of Lubavitch, Brooklyn NY 1977-83

SEFER HAMA'AMARIM 5711, R. Yosef Yitzchak of Lubavitch, Brooklyn NY 1952

SEFER HAMA'AMARIM-BATI LEGANI, R. Menachem M. Schneerson *shalita* of Lubavitch, Brooklyn NY 1977

SEFER HAMITZVOT R. SAADIA GAON, ed. R. Yerucham F. Perla, Jerusalem 1973

SEFER HASHLAMAH AL MINCHAT CHINUCH, New York 1952

SEFER HA'ARACHIM - CHABAD, Brooklyn NY 1970 *e.s.*

SHA'AR HAKAVANOT, R. Chaim Vital, Tel Aviv 1962

SHA'AR HAMITZVOT, R. Chaim Vital, Tel Aviv 1962

SHA'AR MAAMAREI RAZAL, R. Chaim Vital, Tel Aviv 1961

SHA'AR RU'ACH HAKODESH, R. Chaim Vital, Tel Aviv 1963

SHA'AREI KEDUSHAH, R. Chaim Vital, Horodna 1793

SHA'AREI ORAH, R. Joseph Gikatilla, Jerusalem 1960

SHA'AREI ORAH, R. Dov Ber of Lubavitch, Brooklyn NY 1956

SHEVET MUSSAR, R. Elijah of Smyrna, Warsaw 1889

SHIVCHEI HABESHT, ed. Y. Mundshein, Jerusalem 1982

SHNEI LUCHOT HABERIT, R. Isaiah Horowitz, Jerusalem 1963
SHULCHAN ARUCH ARIZAL, Jerusalem 1961
SIDDUR IM DACH, R. Shneur Zalman of Liadi, Brooklyn NY 1965
TANYA, R. Shneur Zalman of Liadi, Brooklyn NY 1965
TESHUVOT RADVAZ, R. David ibn Abi Zimra, New York 1967
TESHUVOT RASHBA, R. Shelomoh ben Avraham Aderet, Bnei Berak 1958
TOMER DEVORAH, R. Mosheh Cordovero, Jerusalem 1969
TORAH OR, R. Shneur Zalman of Liadi, Brooklyn NY 1954
TORAT CHAYIM, R. Dov Ber of Lubavitch, Brooklyn NY 1974
TORAT HASHEM TEMIMAH, R. Mosheh Nachmanides, ed. Chavel, Jerusalem 1963
TORAT SHOLOM, R. Sholom Dov Ber of Lubavitch, Brooklyn NY 1957
TORAT SHMUEL-5629, R. Shmuel of Lubavitch, Brooklyn NY 1958
TZAFNAT PANE'ACH, R. Yaakov Yosef of Polnoy, New York 1954
TZAVA'AT HARIVASH, Anthology of Teachings of R. Israel Baal Shem Tov, ed. Kehot, Brooklyn NY 1982
URIM VETUMIM, R. Jonathan Eybeshitz, Jerusalem 1961
YAD MALACHI, R. Malachi Hakohen, Berlin 1857
YOM-TOV SHEL ROSH HASHANAH, R. Sholom Dov Ber of Lubavitch, Brooklyn NY 1971
ZICHRQN ZOT, R. Yaakov Yotzchak of Lublin, Lublin 1890
ZIVCHEI SHELAMIM, R. Mosheh Cordovero, Jerusalem 1883

Index of Biblical and Rabbinic Quotations

Genesis
1:1 50
2:7 212
15:14 195
28:2 106
28:17 115
46:3 194
46:4 195

Exodus
14:10 168
14:31 113
16:7f. 108
18:16 113
18:19 113
18:20 158
19:6 54
23:5 27,35
25:8 66

Leviticus
19:16 28
19:17 23,28,38,207
19:18 . 22,23,24,26,35,45,47,52, 56,69,73,74,189
21:17f. 59,72,134

Numbers
11:29 63
12:3 119
15:39 146
16:1f. 116
21:5 113
23:21 71

Deuteronomy
4:22 175
5:5 113
6:4 66
6:5 53,189
6:13 114
7:6 51
11:22 95
13:5 212
13:9 35,36
14:1 46,51,52,55,187
14:2 51
15:18 123
20:3 142
28:47 130,131,150
32:2 46
32:9 73
32:47 140

Judges
20:11 60

I Samuels
2:8 88
16:14ff. 150

II Samuels
6:16 130
6:22 130

II Kings
3:15 150

Isaiah
1:4 46
2:3 100

221

11:9 79
14:14 212
29:22 39
33:14 144
52:3 78
55:1 172
58:7 191,194
63:9 51
66:4 149

Jeremiah
4:22 64,118
15:19 110
23:29 172

Ezekiel
1:26 71,146
33:11 33

Hosea
2:1 46
6:3 100

Michah
7:18 51

Habakuk
2:4 213

Zephaniah
3:9 60

Malachi
2:6 111
2:10 55,58
3:12 210

Psalms
1:3 97
2:11 135
19:9 131
31:19f. 117
32:10 149
37:23 195
73:26 66
86:4 142
89:16 122,123
89:48 117
91:15 64
100:2 140,146
103:19 108

104:35 43
112:7 144
118:20 111
119:50 147
128:2 123
139:21f. 27,28,38
139:22 39
148:14 51

Proverbs
3:6 121
3:18 176
4:23 60
6:23 198
8:13 27,46
9:8 32
10:12 69
10:25 87,103,105
13:20 94
14:34 189
17:26 120
19:21 97
20:27 197
22:2 188
25:6 130
28:14 144
29:13 188

Job
3:23 72
3:25 144
5:7 212
11:11 72

Song
4:4 121
4:7 72
5:2 64
8:7 71

Ecclesiastes
1:6 65
4:12 188
5:9 78
7:20 86

I Chronicles
29:11 104,108

TALMUD

Berachot
- 7a 86,120
- 8a 56,163
- 10a 43
- 12b 93
- 14b 167
- 17b 92,105
- 30b 135
- 32a 93
- 34b 90,110
- 51b 98
- 54a 87
- 55a 159
- 57a 47
- 60a 144
- 63b 144
- 64a 98

Shabbat
- 30b 150
- 31a 68,172,207
- 88b 118
- 116a 27,40
- 119a 69
- 133b 175,212
- 149b 120

Eruvin
- 6a 193
- 13b 98
- 19a 47
- 46b 47
- 100b 193

Pesachim
- 22b 114
- 50b 168
- 68b 158
- 113b 27

Yoma
- 9b 67,78,188
- 36b 47
- 38b 88
- 82a 193

Rosh Hashanah
- 16b 120

- 32a 159

Sukah
- 14a 92
- 21b 110
- 45b 87
- 56b 96

Ta'anit
- 3b 115
- 7a 144
- 8a 56,91
- 10a 115
- 16a 114
- 19a 90
- 23a 90
- 23b 114
- 24a 96
- 24b 92,105

Megilah
- 6b 213
- 28b 95
- 29a 67

Moe'd Katan
- 16b 90
- 17a 95

Chagigah
- 5a 71
- 12b 87
- 13a 147
- 27a 47

Yevamot
- 53b 144
- 105a 188
- 109b 188

Ketuvot
- 77b 193
- 111b 95,175

Sotah
- 34b 114

Gitin
- 57b 52
- 70a 132

Kidushin
- 30b 172

32b 95
36a 46
40a 85
40b 86
70a 197

Baba Kama
2a 173
17a 172
92b 96

Baba Metzi'a
31a 208
32b 34
48b 27
62a 25

Baba Batra
17a 86
116a 91

Sanhedrin
29a 36
44a 47
46a 64
93a 99
99a .41,42

Makot
10a 78
23b 161
24a 21

Shevu'ot
39a 56

Avodah Zara
3a 50
3b 62
10b 115

Avot
1:6 93
1:12 39
1:17 214
2:2 188
2:5 177
2:17 121
4:1 197
4:2 161
4:10 60
5:1 159
5:16 75

6:2 194

Avot deR. Nathan
ch. 8 93,96
ch. 11 123
ch. 12 111
ch. 16 .27

Menachot
65a 63

Chulin
7a-b 96
92b 87
110a .193

Bechorot
38b 69

Arachin
11a 150
16b 31,207,208

Temurah
16a 188

Nega'im
2:5 69,197

Nidah
17a 198

Yerushalmi

Berachot
4:4 194
9:1 112
9:5 86

Shevi'it
4:3 115

Bikurim
3:3 100

Shekalim
5:1 32

Betza
5:2 98

Sukah
5:1 150

Mo'ed Katan
2:3 98
3:1 98

Chagigah
1:2 71

INDEXES

Nedarim
  9:4 22,54

Avodah Zara
  2:3 87

MIDRASHIM

Mechilta
  Shemot (on Exodus 3:2)* 51
  Pis'cha:14 (on Exodus 12:41) 51, 67
  Beshalach II:6 (on Exodus 14:31) 113
  Shirta:6 (on Exodus 15:7) 52,187
  Shirta:9 (on Exodus 15:13) . 101, 107
  Bachodesh:1 (on Exodus 19:2) 77
  Bachodesh:3 (on Exodus 19:11) 62
  Bachodesh:4 (on Exodus 19:21) 61

Mechilta deRashby
  Exodus 3:2 51
  Exodus 12:41 51
  Exodus 19:6 54,202

Sifra on Leviticus
  19:17 24,31,208
  19:18 22,207
  26:8 56

Sifre
  Beha'alotecha:84 52,67,187
  Beha'alotecha:87 79
  Devarim:1 31
  Va'etchanan:32 87,135
  Ekev:40 115
  Ekev:42 115
  Ekev:47 85,99
  Ekev:49 95,175
  Re'ey:96 46
  Re'ey:123 123
  Tetze:252 196
  Berachah:343 95

Tanchuma
  Bereishit:1 50,159

Vayera:9 97
Vayera:13 87
Vayera:19 85
Vayishlach:2 85
Mishpatim:7 208
Kedoshim:10 114
Nasso:16 158
Chukat:23 102
Pinchas:11 209
Shoftim:4 93
Nitzavim:1 78

Tanchuma-Kadum
  Bereishit:3 50
  Bereishit:10 50
  Bereishit:21 97
  Vayetze:16 90
  Va'eira:22 90

Bereishit Rabba
  1:1 50,159
  1:4 50
  1:6 50
  3:37 92
  14:4 90
  17:4 212
  24:7 22
  33:3 92
  39:11 97,98
  49:18 87
  53:14 91
  56:7 88,91
  74:3 88
  78:7 123

Shemot Rabba
  2:5 64
  18:5 117
  21:5 168
  34:1 140
  42:9 93

---

  * ed. Friedmann, p. 119b

Vayikra Rabba
- 2:5 52
- 4:6 55,202
- 26:7 71
- 36:4 39,50

Bamidbar Rabba
- 2:15 47
- 3:1 88
- 14:4 90
- 19:28 102
- 21:15 209

Devarim Rabba
- 7:9 62
- 11:9 117

Ruth Rabba
- Petichta:3 52

Shir Rabba
- 1:2 95
- 1:3 101
- 5:2 64,66
- 7:8 87

Kohelet Rabba
- 5:9 78

Midrash Tehilim
- 1:15 87
- 1:19 97
- 2:2 92
- 4:4 51
- 16:11 119
- 19:17 92
- 77:1 92
- 86:1 119
- 100:3 133,135
- 104:27 44

Midrash Mishlei
- ch. 1 110
- ch. 13 94

Pirkei deR. Eliezer
- ch. 16 158
- ch. 19 191
- ch. 25 94

Mishnat R. Eliezer
- ch. 15 99

Pessikta Rabbaty
- Ki Tissa 52,187

Yehudah Veyisrael 97

Pessikta Zutrata (Lekach Tov)
- Genesis 22:11 101

Eliyahu Rabba
- ch. (11)12 55
- ch. 13 191
- ch. 14 50
- ch. 18 24,30,162
- ch. 24 52
- ch. 27 191

Eliyahu Zutta
- ch. 10 52

Yalkut Shimoni
- Balak:766 50
- Devarim:789 31
- Va'etchanan:824 94
- Mishlei:934 77
- Shir:992 97
- Eichah:1034 162

Midrash Hagadol on
- Genesis 18:19 95
- Genesis 28:17 115

Zohar

Zohar I
- 5a 50,159
- 24a 50,159
- 25a 101
- 31a 104,108
- 45b 90
- 47a 159
- 59a 66
- 88a 161
- 105a 43,93
- 120b 51
- 170a 117
- 204b 93
- 216a 76
- 216b 131,150
- 234a 56,60
- 255a 93

Zohar II
- 5b 115
- 6b 97

11b	101	161a	114
38a	100	219b	51
42a	117	221b	114,115
42b	162	227b*f.*	50
47a	102	231b	66,123
53a	194	234a	115
77a	143	235b	108
90b	159,162	246b	117
93a	150	247a	105
99b	214	260a	164
106b	111	275b	95,96
117b	86	281a	86
119a	73	288a	162
124a	162		
124b	100		
128b	66,100		
128b*f.*	93		
129a	93,191		
151b	115		
162b	213		
163b	100		
184b	146		
204a	159		
255a	131,134		

Zohar III

2a	32		
17a	66		
18b	123		
23b	72		
24b	99		
29b	75		
36b	99		
48a	212		
53b	159,164		
55b	100		
68b	87		
70b	100		
70b*ff.*	114		
71a	78		
73a	52,76,186		
79b	100		
85b*f.*	28		
92b	145		
122a	55,202		
148a	100		

Tikunei Zohar

Intr.:3b	160
Intr.:4a	108
Intr.:17a	159
10:25b	164
13:29a	65,66
21:49b	66
21:50b	87,115
21:52a	66
21:59a	134
25:70a	78
25:70b	65
69:99a	121
69:114a	101
6:145b	120

Zohar Chadash

Noach:23d	117
Vayeshev:29d	188
Shir:64a	171
Shir:74d	77

Sefer Yetzirah

2:2	159
2:3	50

Sefer Habahir

51 (157)	14

Maimonides

Sefer Hamitzvot

I:206	24
II:17-21	35*f.*
II:302	24

Mishneh Torah
Hilchot Yessodei Hatorah
 4:13 96
 5:11 95,119
 7:1 96
 7:4 150
Hilchot De'ot
 1:7 145
 2:1 120,140
 2:4 110
 3:3 121
 ch.5 95
 5:1 110
 5:13 119
 ch. 6 26
 6:1 95
 6:2 95
 6:3 25
 6:6-9 28
 6:8 208
Hilchot Talmud Torah
 1:2 96
 3:6ff. 95
 4:1 95
 6:1 95
Hilchot Avodah Zara
 ch. 1-2 112
 2:3 147
 5:4 .... 35f.
Hilchot Teshuvah
 1:1 133
 2:2-4 133
 3:1 86
 3:8 41
 5:1 213
Hilchot Lulav
 8:15 130

Hilchot Gerushin
 2:20 204
Hilchot Matnot Aniyim
 10:2 55
Hilchot Rotze'ach
 13:14 28
Hilchot Sanhedrin
 11:5 36
Hilchot Mamrim
 3:3 43
Hilchot Evel
 14:1 25,26
Hilchot Melachim
 2:6 115
 3:6 115
 7:15 142,143
Perush Hamishnah
 Sanhedrin ch. 10 38,41,112
Shemonah Perakim
 ch. 2 142
 ch. 3 120,140
 ch. 4 145
 ch. 5 150
 ch. 8 142
 Chulin 1:2 43
Moreh Nevuchim
 III:45 150
Kovetz Teshuvot Ve'Igarot . 93,119

Shulchan Aruch

Orach Chayim 156 29,30
 608 29
Yoreh De'ah 245 191
 335 91
Choshen Mishpat 7 46
 272 28,34

Index of Subjects

Aaron
disciples of A. 39
Aaron of Karlin, R. 129
Abraham 98
Action . . . . 72,166*ff.*
affects everything 145
better than sighing 207
good a. always effective 207
see *Mitzvah, act of m.*
Activism 72,183,199*ff.*,214
Adam 71
Adam — edameh laElyon 212
Adler, Dr. Alfred 210
Admonition . . . . 27*f.*
see Rebuke
Ahavah veyirah . .156,165.175.210
wings 164
see G-d, love of G.; Love; *Yirah*
Ahavat chinam 79
Ahavat Yisrael
absorption of 'the one in the
One' 71
active 25
affects all of Israel . . .54*ff.*,64,67
affects *Shechinah* . . . . .65*ff.*,71*f.*
affirmed daily before prayer . .59
A. for *am ha'aretz* 27
A. for peers 26
ahavat chinam 79
association with all Jews . . .59*ff.*
based on common origin 46*f.*,51,
55*f.*,58,74
based on G-d-Israel bond . .49*ff.*
based on Israel's interrelation-
ship . . . . 54*ff.*,58*ff.*
benefits lover and loved . . . 188*f.*
beror lo mitah yafah 35

brotherhood 55
characteristic of Aaron 39
completeness of Israel 59*f.*,61,72
comprehensive principle . . 22,68,
71*ff.*,75
definition of A. . . . . 23*ff.*
directed to reality of soul . .74*ff.*
disregard of others' faults 70
dominant in Chassidism .22,76*f.*
effects Divine effluence . . . . 71*f.*
effort for A. . . . . .188*f.*,207*f.*
elicits attribute of Love . . . . 71*f.*
elicits Divine light 75
errant subject to A. . . . . 43,45*ff.*
exclusions from A. . . . . . 27*f.*,37*ff.*
Gate to G-d 59
Hillel's definition . . . . . 68*ff.*,5*f.*
humility precondition for A. . . .76
interpretation of 'Love G-d' 52*f.*,
17
lack of A. blemishes 59*f.*,64*ff.*,76
leads to love of G-d and
Torah 187
love of G-d 52*f.*,76,186
misguided subject to A. . . 43,47*ff.*
mutual responsibility . . . . . . 56*f.*
negative definition 23*f.*,69
perfection of Israel 59*f.*,71
positive definition 23*f.*,69
prayers for sinners 43
precondition for revelation at
Sinai 77
precondition for ascent of
prayer 59,78
precondition for Messianic redemption . . . . 78*f.*
preconditions70*f.*,75*f.*

229

qualifications of A. . . . . . . .26ff.
redemption through A. 78ff.,188
sinners subject to A. 33ff.,39,43,
   45ff.,61ff.
sinners vs. sin . . . . . 39,42f.,45ff.
to unknown Jews 61,192
universal 61ff.,79,192
whole of the Torah 22,68,71f.,75
wicked subject to A. 33ff.,39,43,
   45ff.,63
see Israel, People of; Jew(s)
Am ha'aretz 27
Am kerovo 51
Amitecha 30
Anavah 129
see Humility
Annus 42,43
Anxiety
can be dispelled 142
dispelled by song150
elicits object of a. 144,149
enticement of *yetzer hara* . . .146
must be avoided 145,146
nullification of a. 143
self-induced a. 142
virtuous a. 144,147
weakens strength of soul 132
Apikores . . . . 27,40,41f.
category no longer applies 45
Arrogance 129
Assistance
material a. 189,191
spiritual a. . . . . .189,190f.
Attributes, Divine A. 72,162,175
Atzvut
arrogance is root of a. 129
avodah zara 129
blemish 134,148
caused by lack of *bitachon* . .138
causes evil dispositions 129f.,134
causes self-indulgence . . . . . 129f.
darkness 134
death 134
dispelled by song and music .150
doorway to forces of evil . . .134

dullness 134
enticement of *yetzer hara* 130,134
evil .134
Gehenom 134
incompatible with love of
   G-d 137
inertia 134
laziness 134
not an explicit sin 128
prevents service of G-d . 130,132
repugnant 130
rooted in self-centeredness . . .129
worse than sin 129
see Anxiety; *Merirut*; *Simchah*
Aveirah .161
see Sin
Awe and Love, see *Ahavah Veyirah*
Bereishit .50
Beror lo mitah yafah 35
Bet Hamikdash, see Temple
Bitachon 137,148f.,201
Bitul Hayesh 108,156
Blemish 56,59,134,148
Body
archetype of b. 58
bodies differ . . . . 75f.
b. secondary . . . . 75f.
Bond
G-d-Israel bond . . . . .49ff.
Chabad . . . 198,199,205,211,212f.
see Lubavitch
Chanina bar Pappa, R. 193
Chanina ben Dosa, R. 89f.,105
Charity
material and spiritual c.189,190f.
Chassid
concerned with others . . . .196ff.
definition of c. . . . . .86,119,196ff.
lamplighter . . . . 196f.
Chassid of the generation 91
Chassidism
demands propagation of Torah
   and *mitzvot* 198
emphasizes proper devotion ..155
emphasizes love 186

INDEXES

emphasizes soul-aspect 176
significance of *Ahavat Yisrael* in
 C. ....22,76*f.*
soul of Torah 76
study of Ch. 145
see *Chabad*; Lubavitch
Chata'im 43
see Sin(s)
Cheerfulness 142,149,150
see *Simchah*
Chessed 86,149
 C. of *Atik Yomin* 149
 rav chessed 149
Chidushei Torah 173
Chinam 78,79
Chochmah 62,108
Choice, Freedom of c. 118
Chotim 43
see Sinner(s)
Chuni Hama'agal 90
Coarseness corrected by Torah 172*f.*
Coins of *tzadik* 97
Community (multitude) vs. Individuals 56
Compromise, danger of c. 205
Confession of sin 57
Control, see Man
Creation, purpose of c. 158
Creatures 39,62,89
 c. reflect Creator 62
Danger 194
Da'at 121,143
Deed, body and soul of deed ..168
Defeatism 201
Devekut
 d. through Torah . 167,175,176*f.*
 emunah 104,113
 perfect d. impossible 175
 see Torah-study
Diversion of thought ... 143*ff.*,148
Divisiveness mutilates .. 66*f.*,72,76
Doctrine
 deliberate distortion of d. 37,41*f.*
 erroneous interpretation of d. 37, 41*ff.*

see Principles of the Faith
Effort ....123*ff.*
Elokah 72
Emunah 137*f.*,210
 devekut 104,113
 leads to *bitachon* 137
Enemy ....27,33*f.*
En Soph 89
Eretz cheifetz 210
Errants led astray 43
Error
 e. in understanding .... 41*f.*
 intellectual e. .... 41*f.*
Essence 187
Etzem 187
Exertion for service of G-d 212
Exile 67,188
Fainteheartedness .... 142*f.*
Fasting 173
Flaws
 overlooking another's f. ..... 70*f.*
 overlooking own f. .... 69*f.*
 seeing another's flaws is seeing one's own 197
Freud, Dr. S. 210
Future 206
Galut, see Exile
Generations, deterioration of g. .32
G-d
 attributes of G. 162,175
 'concentrated' in Torah 159*f.*,163
 creatures of G. 39,59,62
 does not impose impossible burdens 140
 imitatio Dei 175
 immanence of G. 158
 love of G. ....52,186*f.*
 love of G. bound up with love of Israel ....52*f.*,186*f.*
 love of G. implies love of Israel ....52,186*f.*
 love of G. presupposes *emunah*, *bitachon* and *simchah* 137
 love of G. without love of Israel 187

Names of G. 162
senses sorrow of Israel . . 51,64*ff.*
see *Ahavah; imitatio Dei;* Providence; Unity
Gevurah 72
Halachah
   Halachic duties 156,174
   study of *h.* 144,163,170
Hamtakat hadinim 150
Hashgachah Peratit, see Divine Providence
Hate
   blemish . . . . 59*f.*
   evil is to be hated . . . 27*f.*,43,46
   h. in heart most grievous sin . .24
   h. of Israel is hate of G-d 52
   h. of wickedness . .27*f.*,39,43,46
   impersonal 34,46
   mutilates . . . . 59*f.*
   prohibition to h. . . . . .23*ff.*
   see *Sinat chinam*
Health, worries about h. 148
Heretics . . . . .27,37,40,41*f.*
   see *Apikores*
Hezekiah 42
Hillel the Elder 38,68*f.*,75
Hillel, R. 42
Hitlahavut 164*f.*,166*f.*,175
   danger of *h.* . . . . 166*f.*
   touchstone 164
Hoche'ach tochi'ach . . 30*ff.*,38,45, 207
   see Rebuke
Humility 60
   prerequisite for *Ahavat Yisrael* 76
   see Anavah
Idleness 177
Imitatio Dei 175
Improvement through interaction 60
Individual
   every i. counts 61,202
   . .individual responsibility 122*ff.*, 211*ff.*
   like multitude 61
Initiative 200

Intent, purity of i. 155
   see *Kavanah*
Intermediaries . . . . .112*ff.*
Israel, Land of Israel . . . . 114*f.*
Israel, People of Israel
   all souls of I. compound one another 56*f.*,202
   am kerovo 61
   bond with G-d . . . . .49,51*f.*
   children of G-d 46*f.*,51*f.*,55,187
   exile of I. 67
   foundation of world 50,115
   G-d's "twin" 64
   hatred of I. implies hatred of G-d .52
   heart of mankind 115
   individual of I. like multitude 61
   I.-Torah analogy . . . . 77*f.*
   limbs of . . . . .Shechinah 66
   love of I., see *Ahavat Yisrael*
   one body and one soul 54,58,202
   perfection of I. . . . . .56*f.*,59*f.*
   she'er basar 51
   she'erit 51
   surety for one another . . . . . 86*f.*
   term "I." 47
   thought of I. preceded creation 50
   wholeness of I. . . . . 59*f.*
   will never be exchanged 52
   see *Ahavat Yisrael;* G-d; Jew(s); Love of Israel; *Yisrael*
Jerusalem . . . . 114*f.*
Jew(s)
   all J. have part in Torah . . . 77*f.*
   all J. receptive to good 198,202, 204*f.*
   all J. truly like brothers . .55*f.*,74
   cannot separate from Divinity 205
   different kinds of J. 209
   eretz cheifetz 210
   every J. counts 61,202
   interrelationship of J. 54*ff.*,58*ff.*, 202
   see *Ahavat Yisrael;* Israel, People of I.

INDEXES

Joshuah ben Levi, R. . . . . 193*f*.
Joy, see *Simchah*
Judah Hanassi, R. 98
Judaism encompasses everything 206
Judgments
    j. nullified by *simchah* 52
    j. sweetened by *simchah* 52
Kavanah 155,164,166*ff*.,175
Kefirah . . . . .37*f*.,41*f*.
Kibeyachol 160
Knesset Yisrael 67,75
Kofer be'Ikar . . . . 37*f*.
    see *Apikores*; Heretic
Kos shel berachah 98
Lamplighter 196*f*.,209
Legalism 156
Letters of the Torah . . . . . 50,159*f*.
    see Torah
Lishmah . . . . . 156,163*f*.,166,168*f*.
    see *Kavanah; Shelo Lishmah*
Love
    conditional love 75
    l. of G-d, see G-d
    self-love . . . . 69*f*.
Love of Israel
    l. is love of G-d 52,76
    l. portal to courtyard of G-d .59
    to be affirmed daily before
        prayer .59
    universal . . . . .61*ff*.
    see *Ahavat Yisrael*
Lubavitch 183,199
    see *Chabad*
Ma'aseh hamitzvot 166*ff*.,170
    see Action; *Mitzvah*
Mah 108
Maimonides 119
Man
    affected by his deeds 145
    can control his mind . . . . . 143*f*.
Meir, R. 46*f*.,98
Meisit, relationship to *m*. . . . . 35*f*.
Menasya, R. 97
Merirut
    compatible with *simchah* . . .135

differs from *atzvut* . . . . 134*f*.
ferments agitation . . . . 134*f*.
positive 135
sense of contrition 134,135
Mind, diversion of m. . . . 143*ff*.,148
Mitzvah; Mitzvot
    action of *m*. . . . . 156,164*f*.,166*ff*.
    causes joy 131
    even *shelo lishmah* . . . . 168*f*.
    idiom of *tzavta* 161
    mitzvah brings *mitzvah* 161
    thought, speech and deed
        of m. . . . . .167*ff*.
    see *Ma'aseh hamitzvot*; Observance
Modernity 206
Moses 101*f*.,113,116,213
Music 150
    see Song
Mussar, Works of *m*. 170
Mysticism 155
Nachman bar Yitzchak, R. . . 27,36,
    45,46
Names, Divine N., see G-d
Non-orthodox to become
    involved 202
Observance of Torah, partial
    o. . . . . 205*f*.
Offensive vs. Defensive . . . . .199*ff*.
Oral Torah — *Kishutei Kalah* .171
    see Torah; Torah-Study
Orthodoxy 200,206
    failures of o. 200
    obligations of o. 200
    see Non-orthodox
Pardes 96
Pathos, Divine p. . . . . 51,64*ff*.
Persistence . . . . 207*f*.
Personality-cult 211
Peshat
    key to esoterics 171
    understood through *sod* 96
Physicians of the soul 120,122,140
Pikuach nefesh . . . . 192*f*.
Pilpul 171

Pnimiyut 198
Pnimiyut Hatorah 76,171
　see *Peshat*; Torah
Poshei Yisrael 37,47
Poverty, Spiritual p. 191
Prayer
　cannot ascend without *Ahavat Yisrael* 59
　for cheerfulness 142
　for sinners, see Sinner(s)
　plural form 57
　preceded by affirmation of *Ahavat Yisrael* 59
Principles of the Faith 38
　see Doctrine
Propagation of Torah and *Mitzvot* .191,193,198,200,201f.,204f., 207
Providence, Divine P. ...62,192*ff.*, 197,206
Rav 193
Ra'atan .... 193*f.*
Re'acha 26
Rebbe
　lamplighter 209
　not to rely on R. ... 122*ff.*,211*ff.*
　soul-geologist 210
　see *Tzadik*
Rebuke
　mitzvah to rebuke ..28,30*ff.*,207
　requirements for *mitzvah* to r. 31
　see Admonition; *Hoche'ach tochi'ach*
Reciprocity 145,149
Redemption .... 78*f.*
Reishit 50
Responsibility
　for others 211
　individual r. ...... 122*ff.*,211*ff.*
Ru'ach Hakodesh 97,100
　Sadness, see Anxiety; *Atzvut*; *Merirut*
Self-effacement, see *Bitul Hayesh*
Self-love overlooks flaws ..... 69*f.*
Self-neglect 194

Shechinah
　affected by man's behaviour .51, 64*ff.*
　'ailing' of S. 65
　exile of S. 67
　heart of Israel 66
　source of souls 66,71,75
　unity of Holy One, blessed be He, and S. 71,72
She'er basar 51
She'erit 51
Shelo lishmah .... 168*f.*
　see *Lishmah*
Shema 191
Shirayim 98
Shulchan Aruch 144,170
Silence .... 118*f.*
Simchah
　ahavah 137
　all-inclusive attribute 138
　annuls all judgments 150
　compatible with *merirut* 135
　completes a *mitzvah* 132
　elicits Supernal s. 146,149
　energy of the soul 132
　follows *emunah* and *bitachon* 138
　fundamental in Chassidut ...132
　Gan Eden 131
　goodness 131
　holiness 131
　humility goes with s. 129
　kedushah 131
　lack of s. caused *tochachah* ..129
　life 129
　marked by *zerizut* 135
　motivated by song 150
　must be paired with *yirah* ...133
　prayer for cheerfulness 142
　prerequisite to attachment to G-d 132
　pretense of s. to achieve it ...145
　removes all obstacles 150
　s. without *yirah* is frivolity ..133
　test for sincerity .... 131*f.*
　yirah without s. is *marah shecho-*

INDEXES

rah 133
zerizut 135
see Anxiety; *Atzvut; Merirut; Yirah*
Sin(s)
   act of passion .... 37*f*.,41*f*.
   act of rebellion .... 37*f*.,41*f*.
   confession of s. 57
   see Sinner(s)
Sinat chinam .... 67,78*f*.
Sinner(s)
   called "Israel" 47
   children of G-d .... 46*f*.
   full of *mitzvot* 47
   integral part of Israel 46
   obligations toward s. 33*f*.,43
   prayers for s. 43,93
   to be loved and hated simultaneously .... 34*f*.,39,45*ff*.
   to be rebuked 27*f*.,29*f*.,39
   see Wicked
Sod 96
Song 150
Soul(s)
   common source 74
   Divine s. .... 197*f*.
   essence of man 75
   garments of s. 143
   inclusivity of s. 71
   limbs of Shechinah 66
   s. entering body 198
   to be exalted over body .... 75*f*.
Study of Torah, see Torah-study
Success .... 201,207*f*.,213*f*.
Tamati 64
Tefillin 167
Temple destroyed because of *sinat chinam* 67,78
Teshuvah 133,135*f*.,168*f*.,205
   see *Tzadik*
Thought, Faculty of t. 143,149,167, 177
Tochachah 131
Torah
   antidote to *yetzer hara* 172
   blueprint of world 50,159

channel 159
cosmic significance 162,163
Divine Names 162
Divine Attributes 162
enables apprehension of
   Divinity .... 159*f*.
encompasses everything 206
esoteric and exoteric 96
exalts soul over body 75
G-d's garment 160
intermediary 159
letters of T. .... 50,159*f*.
link between G-d and man 158*ff*.
love of T. .... 186*f*.
Oral T. 171,173
pardes 96
peshat .... of T. 96
propagation of T., see Propagation
purifies .... 172*f*.
realistic 140
sod of T. 96
sustains world 159
teaches and instructs ... 158,164
thought, speech and deed
   of T. 167
tool for creation of world ... 159
T. and love of Israel .. 23,68,71,
   72*f*.,75,186*ff*.
T.-Israel analogy .... 77*f*.
unity of G-d and T. ..... 159*f*.
Torah and *Mitzvot* .... 160*ff*.
chitzoniyut of T. 168
hitlahavut for T. 164
intrinsic sanctity of T. ... 166,168
lishmah and *shelo lishmah* 163*f*., 175
medium between G-d and
   man .... 159*ff*.
objective validity of T. . 166,168
pnimiyut of T. 168
precondition for *devekut* 167
precondition for *yirah* 166
propagation of T., see Propagation
Torah-Judaism, offensive
for T. .... 199*ff*.

Torah-study .163*f*.,170*ff*.,175,176*f*.
  gladdens the heart 131,145
  hitlahavut in T. 164
  intense T. 173
  lack of T. . . . . .173,176*f*.
  objective validity of T. 173
  pause in T. for *devekut* . . . 176*f*.
  primary obligation . . 170*ff*.,176*f*.
  rectifies sin and perversions . .173
  see Torah; Torah and *Mitzvot*

Tzadik; Tzadikim
  advice of t. 91,97
  amount of t. 87
  animals of t. 96
  annul Heavenly decrees 90,92,93
  association with t. . . . . .94*ff*.
  attached to Divinity . . . . . .99*ff*.
  baal teshuvah 111
  belief in t. 113
  body of t. holy 99
  called by Name of G-d 100
  central soul . . . . 101*f*.
  channel between Heaven and
    earth . . . . 104*f*.
  characteristics of t. . . . .92*f*.,95*f*.
  coins of t. 97
  compounds world 107
  comprehensive root-soul . . 101*f*.
  concealment of t. 117,123
  concerned about others . . . . 92*f*.
  concerned about sinners 93
  converts judgment to mercy . .92
  counsel of t. 91,97
  decrees of t. confirmed by G-d 90
  definition of term 85
  devekut 104,110
  devoted to Israel . . . . 92*f*.
  Divine holiness attached to t. 99*f*.
  draw forth Divine effluence 105*f*.
  elevate wicked . . . . . . 106,109*ff*.
  elevate world 106
  envied by Satan . . . . 117*f*.
  essential sense of t. 87
  extension of Moses 101
  Face of *Shechinah* 100

figurative sense of t. . . . . . . 86*f*.
foundation of world . 87*f*.,103*ff*.
Gate to G-d 111
gravesites of t. 114
greatness of t. concealed by
  G-d 117
guide and mentor . . . . .120*ff*.
heart of Israel 115
holiness of t. . . . . 99*f*.
humility of t. . . . . 118*f*.
in constant state of *devekut* 109*f*.
intercessor for others . . 90*ff*.,114
intermediary . 104*ff*.,107*f*.,109*ff*.
kol 104,108
kos shel berachah of t. 98
ladder between Heaven and
  earth . . . . 105*f*.
leads people to *teshuvah* 93,106,
  109*ff*.
levels among t. . . . . .85*ff*.
link between Heaven and
  earth . . . . 104*ff*.,108*ff*.
listening to t. 97
looking at t. . . . . 97*f*.
look of t. 98
love G-d's creatures 89
lowering of t. 110
mah .108
material possessions of t. holy 97*f*.
member of King's household . .90
Merkavah 100
mocked . . . . .116*ff*.
Moses 101*f*.,113
mundane involvements of t. .109
neshamah kelalit . . . . 101*f*.
not concerned with self 92
no *yetzer hara* . . . . 86*f*.
obligation to become attached
  to t. . . . . 95,113*f*.
opposition to t. . . . . .116*ff*.
overcome natural order 91
persecution of t. . . . . .116*ff*.
personification of Torah 121
physician of soul 120,122
powers of t. . . . . .90*ff*.

pray for sinners 93
prayer of t. 90*ff*.,114
remainders of t.'s food 98
revilement of t. . . . . .116*ff*.
role-model . . . . 95,120*ff*.
root-souls . . . . 101*f*.
ruach hakodesh of t. 97,100
Sefirah of *Yessod* . . . . 103*f*.
shepherd of people 113
shirayim 98
shvil . . . . .105,114*f*.
sichat chulin of t. 110
soul of t. holy of holies 100
special relationship with G-d .90
spirituality of t. 104
stars in heaven 99
stature of t. 99
superior to ministering angels .99
supernatural abilities 91
talpiyot . . . . 120*f*.
teshuvah . . . . 93,106,110*f*.
thaumaturgic powers of t. 91
theomorphic attributes . . . 100*f*.
thoughts of *teshuvah* induced by t. 106
tzadik hador 88,103
tzadik vera lo 86
tzadik vetov lo 85
t. will not punish . . . . 119*f*.
tzadik yessod olam 87*f*.,103
tzinor . . . . .105,114*f*.
wicked elevated by t. . . . .93,109*f*.
withdrawal of t. 123
world 107
Yessod . . . . 103*f*.
Tzibur 86
Tzimtzum 159

Tzinor . . . . .105,109*f*.
Unity of G-d 160
Unity of G-d and Israel 52,71
Unity of G-d and Torah . . . . 159*f*.
Unity of G-d, Torah and Israel . . . . .186*ff*.
Unity of the Holy One, blessed be He, and Shechinah . . . . .71,72*f*.
Unity of Israel
  u. precondition for giving of Torah 77
  u. precondition for Messianic redemption 78*f*.,188
  see *Ahavat Yisrael*
Warfare, not to be fainthearted in w. . . . . 142*f*.
Wicked
  concern for w. 28,33*ff*.,43
  sufferings of w. 132
  to be hated 27*f*.,35
  to be loved . . . . 34*f*.,39,45*ff*.
  to be rebuked 27*f*.,29*ff*.,39
  two types of w. . . . . 37*f*.
  see *Apikores*; Heretics; Sinner(s)
Will, all depends on w. 213
Yehudah, R., and R. Meir . . . 46*f*.
Yetzer hara 34,86*f*.,172,177
  two forms of y. 172
Yirah
  Torah and *mitzvot* prerequisite for y. .166
  Y. with *simchah* 133
  Y. without *simchah* 133
Yisrael
  acrostic of Y. 77
  term Y. 47
Zerizut, mark of *simchah* 135

לזכות

כ"ק אדמו"ר שליט"א

יהי רצון שהשי"ת יאריך ימיו ושנותיו
בנעימים מתוך בריאות הנכונה
ויצליחו בהנהגת עם ישראל בכלל
וקהל עדת החסידים בפרט
ויוליכנו לקראת משיח צדקנו
בגאולה האמיתית והשלימה
בקרוב בימינו ובעגלא דידן ממש

◆

נדפס על ידי

יעקב עמנואל בן שרה שאשע
רחל בת יטלא אסתר

אלחנן אביגדור בן פריידא זיסל
יהודית אוריה בת רחל
ובניהם **לוי יצחק, אהרן יחזקאל, דוב יהודה**

יצחק יהונתן בן רחל
חנה בת טשערנא רייזל

יוסף בנימין בן רחל
חנה שרון בת רחל

ישראל עובדיה בן רחל